FROM PURPOSE TO
PROMISE
DRIVEN
LIFE

A Prescription For Making The Difference You Were Born To Make

Therman E. Evans, M.D., Ph.D.

ISBN: 978-0-9789508-8-0 $15.95

To learn more about and/or request other
publications by Dr. Therman Evans
please contact the website:
drthermanevans.com or write to
1009 Chandler Avenue, Linden, NJ 07036

This book is one of a series of "Prescriptions" to maximize one's life utilizing an approach that includes the "whole" human being, spirit, mind, and body.

DEDICATION

This book is dedicated to God, my family and God's family everywhere.

Cover: Art and Design by Jean Clervois
VIVID GRAFX (908) 964-0928

TESTIMONIALS

"There are motivational speakers with self-help books and there are books that actually help you to help yourself. *From Purpose to Promise Driven Life* is a powerful, engaging, life-changing book that will immediately captivate you. I hope you continue to get speaking engagements because you're one of the few I've heard in recent years that tell it like it is with real substance."
**- Congressman Edolphus "Ed" Towns
10th District, New York**

"Dr. Evans is a powerful speaker, an inspirational man and a good friend. He believes in his purpose and promises in life and is driven to succeed while helping others at the same time. His latest book makes powerful parallels about problem-driven, purpose-driven and promise-driven individuals. Regardless of your religious affiliation or situation, this book is a must read. I highly recommend Dr. Evans in any aspect."
**- Glenda F. Hodges, PhD. JD.
Howard University College of Medicine**

"….simple and profound or, 'simply profound' was my first reaction to Dr. Evans' grasp of what life and living is really all about."
- Dr. Camille Alleyn, Windsor, CT

"Dr. Evans is a marvelous human being, and a supremely gifted speaker and writer. He sets out to heal the world with his message and ministry. True healing can only occur by attending to the mind, body and spirit."
- Robert H. Williams, MD
Senior Attending Physician, Howard
University Hospital

"With divine insight and revelation, Dr. Therman Evans moves us from problems, through purpose, and finally directs the reader, step-by-step, to the sacred confines of *promise driven life.* In this book, we learn to live bigger, better and beyond human imagination. There are healing prescriptions on every page for our liberation and transformation. I've been waiting for the next level after *purpose,* and here it is! Now, we can bravely stand on the promises and not just the premises of problems. Dr. Evans makes us understand that *purpose* without *promise* is success without the source (GOD)."
Dr. Gwendolyn Goldsby Grant,
Former Advice Columnist—ESSENCE
MAGAZINE, Multimedia Psychologist,
Inspirational Speaker, and author of
"The Best Kind of Loving."

"Reading this book has been a blessing to me in many ways. In the challenging work of leading a community, through my responsibility as Mayor of the Borough of Roselle, *"Purpose to Promise"* is a road map to success for me and any leader attempting to create a vibrant and productive community in these very difficult times. We are lead to raise the bar and focus on the vision of new promise. As we develop as leaders from *purpose to promise* we take the community with us as our influence and prosperity grow through commitment and accountability. I want to thank Dr. Therman Evans for this powerful work which will be a life changing paradigm for individuals, families, communities and nations for years to come."

- Mayor Garrett Smith, Borough of Roselle, NJ

"Thank you for the book. What I have read so far is very personally encouraging and insightful as I think about my life and work here. I'm looking forward to taking in the rest."

- Pastor Bill Flug
United Methodist Church of Westford
Westford, MA

"This book should be required reading for anyone who's serious about living their best possible life."

- Dale Kelly, Principal, I.S. 364 Gateway
Brooklyn, NY

"I can't begin to tell you what *From Purpose to Promise Driven Life* has meant to me. This book has made a profound difference in my life. After reading the chapter on How to Discover/Uncover Your Promise, I have to tell you it has to be one of the most powerfully written -- guided by the spirit of God. Dr. Evans, every chapter in your book will touch someone. Your book needs to be read by all! Be Blessed Always!"
- Andre Hollis, Principal
New Horizons Community Charter School
Newark, NJ

"First of all, thank you! God knew that I needed this book, and you were listening when He asked you to give it to me. I have been reading and re-reading the opening chapters, and have spent a week on the first day's 'challenge.' I have been in Problem Quicksand…that's an ugly truth, but the first step in solving a difficulty is to recognize it, right?"
- Debbie Botham, businesswoman
Chelmsford, MA

"This book has challenged and motivated me to do things that I thought I could never do or would do. I never thought that I would be a part of a reading group, because I never was the one who read books for pleasure. The easy readings and activities enticed me to not only want to enhance my spiritual walk with God and live a promise driven life, but to help others as well.... The book has also motivated me to ask my boss about ways to develop my career opportunities. The conversation with my boss led to doors opening that I didn't think about opening. This book has truly blessed me to believe in myself and to strive to be the best at whatever I do."

- Laynnea Jones, L'Oréal USA

"Joy and liberation is what I felt as I read this wonderful book. It's so rich, so powerful. I wish everyone who is looking for a transformation would read this book. Get a revelation! Awesome! Dr. Evans is so transparent in the book; you can sense the blood, sweat and tears poured into this wonderful work. I can't wait to see what else you have in that creative mind of yours. You have been a blessing to me. Be ready to receive when you read this book."

- Stan Neron, Director
Office of Youth Services, Elizabeth, NJ

"I am glad that I was deemed worthy to have the opportunity to meet Dr. Evans, and to have the chance to buy a copy of this book to share with others. 'Each of us is born with a great amount of innate potential. The full achievement of this potential (promise/dream/vision) brings with it the appropriate and commensurate glory.' Don't despair....Where you are now is a part of the journey you must travel on your way to the future that God has destined for you. Ahead of you is health, wealth, prosperity, and favor. Ready, get set...go! Dr. Evans will show you how."

- Rev. Darnice Jones
Gethsemane Baptist Church
Brooklyn, NY

CONTENTS

Prologue

Writing this book has had a transformational impact on me. My perspective on life is different. My decisions are different. The challenges I seek and take on are different. Conversations with myself and others have a different focus. Desired goals, objectives and impacts are much better, bigger and broader than they used to be. Now, in all I attempt to do I want to be and make the difference I was born to make.

My thoughts, feelings and behaviors now revolve around not just making an impact or leaving a footprint, but making **the** difference that leads to the liberation and maximization of the lives of my family, friends and others.

I am now committed to more than just God's purpose for my life. I am driven by God's promise for my life. My prayer and hope is that it will do the same for you. Though I did not start out with any preconceived number, plan or formula in mind, as it turns out, a suggestion of one emerged. What emerged is a forty-nine day transformational journey to promise driven life. (Chapter Six) If you follow and adhere to the principles and steps outlined in this book, your life will be transformed. Several points are important to this journey.

1. From day one to day forty-nine the suggestions are additive. That is, it is very important to master the step/principle of

1

each week, and then, add to it the step/principle of the next week. For example, achieving and practicing the step/principle of maturity does not replace practicing the steps/principles of commitment, accountability and preparation, but is added to them. The process is progressive and additive.

2. Each step/principle stands alone and can be used to strengthen or enhance your life in that particular area. My belief is that you will best benefit from this book by starting from the beginning. If you are already clear about what God's promise is for your life you may start where you feel you need the most help.

3. It is important to master each step/principle and not just select the ones you are comfortable with. Implement the plan for each day of each step/principle. Be mindful that it may take you much longer than a day to successfully accomplish what is suggested for any particular day. In fact it may take many days. This is just fine. Don't stress out about it, keep pushing, it's a journey.

4. Don't be in a hurry. Enjoy the journey. Savor each step. Experience the excitement. Track and treasure the transformation.

5. The number seven and multiples of the number seven occur quite frequently in scripture. The Hebrew word for seven is

sheba or shibah, which comes from the word shaba, which means to be complete, to feed until full, to swear or take an oath. The significance of the number seven includes the following:

a) Genesis 2:1-3, "By the seventh day God had finished the work He had been doing; so on the seventh day He rested from all His work. And God blessed the seventh day and made it holy, because on it He rested from all the work of creating that He had done."

b) Jubilee is a word in Hebrew that means to flow, to bring forth, to carry, to lead forth. It also means the continuous blast of a horn, the signal of the silver trumpets, a trumpet, or a festival.

c) After every 49 years (seven times seven years), the 50th year was declared a year of Jubilee or liberation. Leviticus 25:8-13

d) Pentecost, the festival which takes place seven weeks on the fiftieth day after the Passover, was the occasion when the promised gift of God's Holy Spirit descended upon the gathered disciples who were then and thereby empowered and enabled to achieve their promise of reaching

3

everybody everywhere with the message of Jesus the Christ.

e) The walls of Jerusalem were rebuilt by Nehemiah and the people in just over seven (52 days) weeks.

f) Seventy (10 times 7 years) years was the time of exile prescribed by God. After seventy years, the people would be given access back into their promised land.

g) Each year of 365 days has in it approximately seven seven-week (actually 52 days) periods.

h) The festival of unleavened bread, celebrating the exodus from Egypt (slavery and limitation) to a new way of living in the land of promise, was seven days long.

i) The festival of shelters/tabernacles, celebrating God's protection and guidance through the wilderness, lasted for seven days and took place in the seventh month of the year.

j) Jesus uses the number seven to indicate the importance of harboring no malice or grudges and being completely forgiving all the time, when He says people should be forgiven "seventy times seven" times. Matthew 18:22 (King James Version, KJV)

4

    k) The Sabbath Day or Seventh Day is the promised blessed day of rest, repose, and celebration in God, and what He has done for us, in us and through us.

6. There is always benefit to a group experience. You may want to read this book along with your family, ministry, church, business, organization or friends. The group can help encourage, inspire, support and/or make suggestions for specific activities.

7. Please provide me with testimonial feedback as you travel this transformational journey and do encourage others to take the trip as well. God bless you. I look forward to hearing from you and may your experience be magnificent.

INTRODUCTION

Promise is defined as 1) an agreement to do or not to do something; 2) an indication, as of a successful future; and 3) a basis of expectation. Essentially, the word promise speaks to two related concepts: a) a pledge, covenant, commitment, security, agreement; and b) potential, possibility, that can be, that can happen, that can be known, that can be achieved, capability, ability. These two concepts are recognized and harmonized in scripture where God – the overarching, creative intelligence and power of the universe – speaks to and through humankind. In other words, the promise (pledge, covenant, commitment, security, agreement) of God is/represents the promise (potential, possibility, capability, ability, what can be) of man. **The mechanism by means of which this is manifested is the movement of the spirit of God in man.**

Since God is completely integrous and whole, the Spirit of God is the Word of God. The Word of God is the Spirit of God. In John 6:63 Jesus says, "…the words I speak to you are spirit and life." Genesis 1:1-3 says, "In the beginning God – the overarching, creative intelligence and power of the universe – created the heaven and the earth. The earth was without form, empty and filled with darkness. And the spirit of God moved … and God said, let there be…" These verses of scripture speak to the integrity between the spirit of God and the Word of God. When the spirit of God moves, God speaks. God speaks what is in His spirit. Since God's wholeness and integrity must include His actions as well, what God speaks, God does.

In scripture then, a promise of God comes from the spirit of God, which is the Word of God, which is the power of God, which gets the results of God. In short, the promises of God are the results of God for those who live promise driven lives.

Promise is an agreement to do something.

Promise is an assurance that something will be done.

Promise is the expression of certainty regarding a future possibility.

Promise is a present guarantee of something not yet done.

Promise is only as good as the promiser.

Promise is only as guaranteed as the guarantor.

Promise is only as sound as the promiser.

Promise is only as certain as the promiser.

Nothing is more good, guaranteed, sound or certain than God. In fact, God is so good, so sound, so certain, that His promises are already done, guaranteed and available to those who decide and determine to live a promise driven life.

While the love of God is available and accessible to anybody and everybody, the promises of God are available and accessible only to those who obediently practice the principles attached.

God gives nothing on a silver platter, but everything He promises, He guarantees, provided it is pursued in the appropriate way.

God is a promise driven God; God is driven by His promise; and God's promise is God's Word. God is driven to achieve His promise – His Word – for His people. The promise of God includes the purpose of God. The purpose of God is in the promise of God. Outside of His promise it is impossible to ponder the purpose of God.

Isaiah 55:8-11 explains that God operates at a much higher level than we do. **The highest level from which you can work is the level of promise.** This is the level of great or highest results, fruit, success, positive outcome, effects and impact. For God, the level of promise is prosperity, abundance, overflow, treasure and wealth. **God's Word is God's full potential.** What God says, God does to its fullest, at its highest and best. When God speaks, all of God is speaking. When God speaks, there is no equivocation, no back and forth, no hot and cold, no wishy-washyness, no maybeness, and no perhaps. **When God speaks there is only promise.** And because God's thoughts and ways are much higher than ours, His promise comes forth to us as magnificent manifestation, plenteous prosperity and, abundance and overflow. God is good. Life is good. **God is life in abundance. All of God's promises**

speak to great and highest fruit, increase, sufficiency, productivity, abundance, prosperity, and overflow. All of God's promises are manifested in the life of Jesus the Christ. 2 Corinthians 1:20 says, "For no matter how many promises God has made, they are 'Yes' in Christ..." (New International Version, NIV)

God is a promise driven God. All of God's promises have principles attached. When you practice the principle, you achieve the promise. Jesus, the Christ is the principle to all of God's promises. The challenge is to model Jesus, to practice the principles of Jesus.

The pattern, practice and productivity of a promise driven life is initially outlined in Genesis but is repeated on a number of occasions throughout the Bible. It is a seven-step process that takes us from a problem driven, unproductive, dysfunctional, existence of shapelessness, emptiness and darkness, to a magnificent life-supporting and life-promoting structure of order and organization called the universe. Briefly stated, the seven steps are:

1) "The Spirit of God Moved ..."
Commitment

Your promise (full potential), dreams/visions reside in and come from the realm of the spirit. The spirit is the strongest most powerful part of the human being. And so, it stands to reason that's where the picture of "all you can be" (your promise) would come from. When your spirit is moved, the strongest, most powerful part of you is moved. Since your promise, dream/vision represents your highest and best, the movement of your strongest and most powerful self is necessary.

Achievement of promise (highest potential, 'all you can be') requires commitment; it requires total dedication. This is why Jesus was clear that to live His promise of being God on earth He had to "love God with all His heart, all His mind, all His soul and all His strength," Mark 12:30(NIV). In other words, He had to be committed to the promise/dream/vision at the deepest, and most powerful level, the spirit.

Real commitment is spiritual. Unless commitment takes place in your spirit, you're not really committed. And so, the first step in living a promise driven life is commitment. **Commitment means your desire to accomplish what you are committed to must be greater than the desire to avoid what you will have to go through.**

2) "God Said." Accountability
Your promise/dream/vision should be clear, declared and expressed in writing even if to no one but yourself. Habakkuk 2:2-3 says, "Write down

10

the revelation (vision) and make it plain on tablets so that a herald may run with it. For the revelation (vision) awaits an appointed time; it speaks to the end and will not prove false. Though it lingers, wait for it. It will certainly come and will not delay." An old proverb says, "If you don't know where you are going, any road you take will get you there." Writing down and speaking your promise/dream/vision is important for the following reasons:

a. Repetition – **affirmation** – is the essence of learning. The more you recite, repeat and affirm it, the more clear and real it becomes to you.

b. It establishes jurisdiction and **authority.** It says, you have decided and determined to take charge of your life and move it in the direction of its full potential.

c. It outlines the necessary **action** and activity pathways that must be traveled to accomplish the promise/dream/vision.

d. It creates private and public **accountability**.

When you speak your promise/dream/vision from God, you are saying to yourself and others, this is what I want to be held accountable for. This is what I am working on and towards. This is what I want to be judged against. This is what I want to be known as. God is the ultimate when it comes to accountability. **What God says is what He**

does. What God does is who He is. Since God is driven by His Word/promise, He is totally accountable.

3) "Let There Be….." Preparation

Achieving promise requires preparation and development. Genesis 1:1 says, "In the beginning God created the heaven and the earth." Then, the rest of Chapter One of Genesis goes on to describe all of the preparations and developments that were necessary to the successful creation of the heaven and the earth. An additional thirty verses are added to verse one to flesh out the preparation for and development of the heaven and the earth. Preparation (training, learning, disciplining, focusing, experimenting) and development are essential to achieving promise.

You cannot just walk into your promise nor will you have your promise/dream/ vision handed to you on a silver platter. Though promised, it will require your most major work effort. And much of that work effort will be in the area of preparation and development. You are limited in what you can cause 'to be' by your preparation and development.

In the parable of the 'Talents' in Matthew 25, Jesus makes clear that we are all gifted in different ways at different levels. And **the impact we can have is a function of how prepared and developed we are.** There were three servants who were given talents based on their ability.

Matthew 25:15 says, "...to one he gave five talents, to another two, and to another one; to every man according to his several ability." Your ability, power, might or strength can be grown through preparation and development. The more prepared you are and the more developed you are, the more you will be able to cause 'to be'. **Promise driven people prepare and develop.** Promise driven people go back to school, pursue degrees, take courses, seek mentors, submit to mentoring, constantly read, and are always doing something in a continuous effort to develop themselves and be prepared to bring into existence their highest and best.

Paul was not one of the twelve originally selected disciples. However, he wrote close to one-half of the New Testament. Why? Preparation and development. Paul was more highly prepared, trained, learned, skilled, disciplined and developed than the original twelve disciples. Acts 22:1-3 says it this way, "Brothers and fathers, listen now to my defense." When they heard him speak to them in Aramaic, they became very quiet. Then Paul said, "I am a Jew, born in Tarsus of Cilicia but brought up in this city. Under Gamaliel I was thoroughly trained in the law of our fathers and was just as zealous for God as any of you are today."

4) "It Was So."   Maturity

Promise driven people are mature. They seem to recognize life's higher agenda and are not only focused on it, but appear to practice it daily. God's promises represent life's higher agenda. God's promises revolve around, and are all relevant to, abundant life. Abundant life is the maturity, readiness and capacity for spiritual strength, health, healing, wholeness, wealth, prosperity and overflow. This is God's promise to us, but it is not just for ourselves. Herein lies the significance of maturity. Babies are immature. A primary characteristic of babies, and therefore immaturity, is self-centeredness. Babies, infants, toddlers, are all about themselves and their immediate gratification. They want what they want and they want it now.

Where everybody, or large numbers of people primarily focus on themselves and the immediate gratification of their needs and wants, you have an immature environment unready for God's promise. It is an atmosphere where you have spiritual babies. This type of atmosphere is characterized by frequent crying, complaining and asking for something to meet individual, personal need. Babies must mature or something is very wrong. Everything must be done for babies. Babies are not mature enough to care for themselves. As babies mature they can care for themselves. When babies are truly mature, ready and at their full capacity they can care for themselves and others as well.

14

Real maturity is a capacity and readiness to care for others. Promise driven people are mature. Promise driven people have a passion for helping others. Promise driven people have the godly quality of being "other" focused on their quest to fulfill their promise/dream/vision.

Nothing is ready until it is ready. The necessary preparation and development must go into what you are causing 'to be' until it is mature and ready to be 'so'. You can recognize the readiness of a promise driven life by the maturity reflected in concern and care for others in their attitude, decision-making, beliefs, behaviors and habits.

5) "It Was Good..."   Productivity

Promise driven people are productive. They get things done. They are not perfect – (no one is) – but they are productive.

God is the ultimate example of productivity through nature. Nothing known to humans is more productive than nature. Nature is the most life promoting, life supporting and life enhancing entity known. Nature is always good. Nature is always productive. Nature is always supporting, promoting even enhancing life. Even during the worst of storms, tornados, hurricanes, earthquakes, cyclones, tsunami, heat or cold, nature continues to provide life sustaining oxygen, and water and sunshine and soil and food. Even the storms, I'm sure, contribute in some way to a realignment that fosters its productivity.

God is good. Nature is good. Productivity is good. God, nature and productivity are good all the time.

Though sometimes things must be stirred up, shaken up, even broken up for progress to occur, God, nature and productivity are still good.

6) "It Was Blessed." Expansion

Promise driven people do not back away from trial by fire. They do not back away from big challenges. Promise driven people appreciate that big promise, big dreams, big visions, to be achieved, require facing big trials, big tasks and big challenges. To achieve the promise given to them by God, people in scripture had to have the blessing of God. When God blesses people, at least three things are true:

i. It is for something big, major and extremely difficult.

ii. God's help is required to achieve it.

iii. It will alter your environment, change your atmosphere, shift or change your paradigm. That is, it will change the way you do things and the things you do.

When God blesses something, it's going to happen. It's going to happen no matter how big, major, or difficult. It's going to happen no matter how impossible the circumstances or hopeless the situation. Inherent in God's blessing is refinement, enhancement, expansion and promotion. God blesses because God knows you will need His help to achieve the promise/dream/vision He gives. God blesses because God knows His promise/dream/vision is so much bigger than you that He must guarantee it. When God says, "It's blessed", He's saying it's bigger than you, it's more difficult than you can handle, and it's life changing, but, I'm making it happen.

Abraham's life changing journey away from everything familiar to him, to God's promise for him, was bigger than him and more difficult than he could handle on his own, so God blessed it from the start. When the angel came to Mary with the life changing promise/dream/vision which was much bigger than she was, and far beyond her ability to comprehend, he addressed her in verse 28 of the first chapter of Luke as, "Thou who are highly favored, the Lord is with you; blessed are you among women."(KJV) In other words, Mary had to be blessed at the outset to successfully accomplish the promise/dream/vision God gave to her. **Whom God blesses, God is with. Whom God blesses are in need of God's presence to accomplish what God gives to them.**

The accomplishment of the promise/ dream/vision God gives, refines, enhances, expands and promotes the

individual in the direction of abundant life that blesses others. Facing the big trials, tasks and challenges expands you and enlarges your territory.

Promise driven people know they are blessed. They know God is with them. They know they need God's help. They depend on God. They go where God leads.

7) "And, It Was A New Day." The Promise

The promise driven life is a full life. It is a rich (in experience and achievement) life. It is a blessed life. It is a fulfilling life. It is a life of impact. It is a life of progress and productivity. It is a life of growth and creativity. It is a life of favorable results and outcomes. It is a life of improvement, increase, multiplication, plenteousness, prosperity, wealth and overflow.

Promise driven lives change the way things are done. They change the order of things, push the envelope and stretch out the edges. They alter the environment, change the atmosphere and shift paradigms. Promise driven lives enjoy more order and organization as their priorities are clear and clearly understood. They enjoy more love, joy, peace, patience and kindness. They have more faith, righteousness, humility and self-discipline.

God is promise driven. I believe God is calling us to be the same.

I. A BRIEF LOOK AT PROBLEM DRIVEN LIFE

The world tends to be problem focused. So much of the world's time, energy, effort and focus seem to be problem driven.

We are all born into a world full of problems. Though at different times and in different places, we are all born into the same world. Job 14:1 says, "Man born of woman is of few days and full of trouble." Sometimes, like Job, we experience one problem after another, and worse, one problem on top of another. The world is full of problems. Problems are everywhere all the time. Problems come attached to life. Life has problems. It has big ones, little ones, simple and very complicated ones. In life, problems are a constant. There are and always will be problems. In fact, life could be described as an intimate interplay between your problems and how you handle them.

A problem is simply any gap between what you have and what you need or want in any area of your life. For example, if you have five dollars but need or want ten, you have a problem. If you have no car but need or want a car, you have a problem. If you have completed one-half the credits for your college degree but you need or want to achieve your degree, you have a problem. If you have no food, but need or want food you have a problem. If you are 13 years of age but need to be 16 or 18 years of age to be eligible for something, you have a problem. If you have no job or no career, but need or want a job or career, you have a problem. If you live in an apartment but you need or want a house, you have a problem. If you are single but want to be married, you have a problem.

Problems are not only a fact of life and a constant in life, they can also be described as life itself. A problem is a gap, a hurdle, something missing, or a perceived difficulty, hardship, challenge, pain, trial, or trouble. **A problem is anything that requires spiritual, mental or physical effort, energy and work to handle or overcome.** The size of the problem determines the necessary amount of spiritual, mental and physical effort, energy and work.

Many people live their lives based on their problems. The driving force in their life is their problems. They are driven by the number of problems, the kinds of problems, the size of problems, and their frequency. When problems drive your life, you are living a problem driven life. This means your life and its direction are being determined by trouble, trial, pain, challenge, hardship, difficulty, what's missing, what you don't have, gaps and hurdles. Life lived from this perspective is a life always focused on needs. People who are always focused on and talking about what they need or want can be described as 'needy' or self-centered or even selfish. This is a deficit perspective. This is a 'what's wrong' perspective. This is a 'things are never right' perspective. This is a 'there's always something wrong with something' perspective.

People and organizations who live from this perspective frequently do and seek to do **needs** analyses or **needs** assessments. They operate from the assumption, something is missing, and therefore, something is needed to do what needs to be done. And, until it is secured, things won't be right.

Problem driven life is life spent focusing on weakness, shortcoming, what's missing, what you don't have, what you need, what you want. Obviously this approach or perspective can never get you to be your highest, best, strongest or most. And, you'll be working extremely hard.

Problem driven life is reactive. It is defensive. It is always behind. It is always trying to catch up. By definition then, problem driven life is more exasperating. It requires more effort, energy and work. It generates more distress and frustration. And, it makes less progress. Defensive energy is more draining than the energy of offense. In this instance, athletics becomes a metaphor for life. On defense you must spend energy trying to figure out what the opposition is going to do, then figure out what you should do to counteract that, and then you must do it. Whereas on offense, all you have to do is decide what you want to do and do it. Perhaps this is an over-simplification of highly complicated professional sporting strategies, but it is supported by the fact that in football, you only hear concern expressed about the length of time the defense is on the field, not the offense.

Problem driven life focuses on its pain, hardship, trial, trouble and difficulty.

What you pay attention to you grow. Problem driven people focus on their trial, trouble, hardship and difficulty with one goal in mind, Relief! They want relief from the pain. They want the trial to be over. They want the trouble to go away. They want the hardship and the difficulty to be lessened. This of course means that feelings play a significant role in the lives of problem driven people. They want their problem solved. They want relief. They want to feel better.

When you live a problem driven life, once the problem is gone, or you feel better, you return to the behavior that led to the problem in the first place. Then, it's only a matter of time before the same or a similar problem occurs. This is reflected over and over again in scripture.

The fifth chapter of the Book of John describes a man who had been an invalid for 38 years. He lived a life of weakness. He lived a life of dependency. His entire life had been one of lower level living. His daily life revolved around the basic problems of food, shelter and trying to feel better. Each day he congregated with a great number of people challenged by and focused on their own problems. This is a typical "problem driven" environment. Problem driven environments have a host of problems. They have a host of people with a host of problems. And, they have a host of people who are focused on their host of problems. A problem driven environment is one where there are always a host of problems even after one or many are solved. In a problem driven environment, people are focused on themselves and their problems, never or rarely do they focus on others and what would be best for all.

The 'Pool of Bethesda' was a place where people with problems gathered. They had big problems, little problems, simple and complicated ones. Their common theme was, problems. Their problems brought them together. Their problems shaped their lives. Their problems drove their lives. They were all at the pool because of their problems. There is no scriptural evidence to indicate or even suggest they gathered at the pool for strengthening fellowship or strategic planning to help heal or deliver everybody from their problem. They gathered at the pool because the conventional wisdom at the time was, the first one in the pool after its waters were stirred up by an angel would be healed. In other words, the problem of one person would be fixed, while the problems of all the other people remained to be focused on. So, the atmosphere was one where the people went from one problem to another. And, no matter how many problems were solved, there were always more problems. **A problem driven environment is one where everybody's concern is "me", "my", and "mine". A problem driven person is one whose concern is me, my and mine.**

At the pool of Bethesda there were a large number of people with a large number of problems all gathered around the selfish notion of being the first **one** in the pool after its waters were stirred by an angel. The man who had been infirm for 38 years typifies what happens with a problem driven person in a problem driven environment. The man's problem remained for thirty-eight years. The man's environment was the same for thirty-eight years. The man kept going to the same place for thirty-eight years. He kept hanging with and hanging around the same people for thirty-eight years. He kept "waiting" for something outside of him (stirring of water) to happen so he could then react and take advantage of it to fix his infirmity problem.

Problem driven people tend to procrastinate. They tend to wait, hoping somebody will do for them what they should be doing for themselves. **Problem driven people tend to want something for nothing.** They want

24

relief from pain but they don't want to do anything to achieve it. They want a better (problem-free) life, but they don't want to have to work for it. They want their problems fixed but they don't want to have to spend any energy or effort in the process. They want, and will often talk about success, winning, victory and being a champion but, will not initiate and sustain the effort necessary to accomplish them.

Problem driven people make a lot of excuses. They have plenty of rationalization for why things haven't changed and they have remained in the same condition for the past many years. And, they can usually point to and include other people as being at least partly if not totally responsible for their problem.

When Jesus asked the man with the thirty-eight year-long illness, "Do you really want to be well?" the man started answering a different question. He started explaining why he was not yet well. And, the first thing he did was point to others as being responsible for why he was still ill.

This man's life typifies what happens with problem driven people who live problem driven lives. They spend a lot of time, effort and energy waiting for something to happen. They are quite disabled, disconnected, and distressed. They experience high levels of frustration, disappointment, and, are constantly battling discouragement. Further, unless and until they are touched by promise, nothing will change. Fortunately, the final chapter of this man's life was totally different as he was touched by his promise (Jesus). Jesus (the Word/promise of God) came by one day and changed everything.

Another example of a problem driven environment filled with problem driven people is in the second chapter of Exodus. It talks about how the people of Israel moaned and groaned because of their slavery, and they cried to God. Verses 24-25 says, "God heard their groanings and remembered his covenant/promise with Abraham, Isaac and Jacob. And God looked on the Israelites with concern." While the people in slavery were crying and complaining to God about their problems, Moses was on the backside of the desert talking to God about solutions. Moses was a promise driven person. More will be said about promise driven people later.

Problem driven people complain a lot.

They talk about their problems a lot. They rehearse their problems and associated pain over and again. They want people to know what they are going through. They want people to know how difficult things are for them. They want sympathy. They want pity. They want relief! They want to feel better. But, they are not all that interested in changing the way they live. Therefore, their lives rarely change.

God inspired Moses to step up to his promise by allowing God to use him to liberate the people.

Moses received a revelation (burning bush) from God that his people could and should be free. But, the people remained unchanged. Their minds were still enslaved. They were still problem driven. Because they were problem driven, it was only a matter of time before they found another problem about which they could cry and complain. And, sure enough, the people began to find one problem after another.

First, it was Pharoah's army approaching them as they were trapped by the Red Sea. This was a problem about which they cried and complained. Then there was the problem of no water. They cried and complained about that. Then there were the problems of no meat and another occasion of no water. They cried and complained about that. Then, there was Moses' forty-day absence during which he communed with God on the mountaintop. They cried and complained and convinced Aaron to abandon God and build a golden calf idol to worship.

Even at the very edge of the promised land, with tangible evidence of its fertility in hand, they cried, complained and convinced themselves that they were not able to enter. And, they were not able because of all the problems associated with entrance into the land of promise. The big fortified walls were a problem. The big, strong people there were a problem. Their perception of themselves as too little and too small grasshoppers was a problem. Every way they turned and everywhere they looked, they saw problems. And, because they saw nothing but problems all around them, they cried, complained and convinced themselves they were not able to achieve their promise and worse, should return to slavery. Numbers 14:1-4 outlines the painful yet typical reaction to adversity of problem driven people.

That night all the people of the community raised their voices and wept aloud. All the Israelites grumbled against Moses and Aaron, and the whole assembly said to them, "If only we had died in Egypt! Or in this desert! Why is the Lord bringing us into this land only to let us fall by the sword? Our wives and children will be taken as plunder. Wouldn't it be better for us to go back to Egypt?" And they said to each other, "We should choose a leader and go back to Egypt." (NIV)

Problem driven people go from problem to problem with a priority focus on relief, or at least finding the pathway of least resistance. They don't want to change but they want their problems to go away. **Problem driven people cry and complain about problems, don't want problems, don't want the problem of fixing problems and yet they are always focused on problems. Problem driven people experience extremely slow and little progress and never achieve their promise.**

Too many people are living problem driven lives. They are never where they want to be and never doing what they want to do. They are always behind, always trying to catch up and always reacting. They are virtually always on defense, always distressed, sometimes depressed and frequently fatigued or plagued by not having enough energy.

Problem driven people can always find something wrong or something missing and focus on it. They rehearse and blow up hardship, difficulty, pain, trial, trouble, hurdles, gaps and lack. **Problem driven people are deeply rooted in slavery mindsets, victims' values, poverty perceptions, and negative attitudes.** And, as has already been stated, they never reach their promise.

Problem driven life is essentially all about "me". Its focus is limited to "me" and "my" concerns.

Purpose driven life is about me, why I'm here, how I fit with others, and why they are here. Its focus is broader and more positive.

Promise driven life is all about us and how we do our best to benefit the most.

Only you know what drives your life. But, I know you don't have to live according to your problems, you can live according to your promise.

I have tried to outline a prescriptive pathway for promise driven life. As you read this prescription, let it help you examine where you are and inspire you to begin the journey to 'all you can be'.

If you are ready to discover and begin making the difference you were born to make, decide to follow this prescription and get started on the most magnificent journey of your life.

II. A BRIEFER LOOK AT PURPOSE DRIVEN LIFE

People who know their purpose have meaning and direction in their lives. They have goals and objectives. They have something to live for. People living purpose driven lives are living at a much higher level than those whose lives are driven by problems. If you know you are living a problem driven life, decide today to change. What sense does it make to decide to live your life as a victim or a loser. Decide to be victorious. Decide to be the winner. After all, it's your life. Find your purpose. Everybody and everything on earth has a purpose. What's yours? When you find your purpose your life changes. Rick Warren in his wonderful book "The Purpose Driven Life", (Zondervan 2002) does a masterful job in guiding people to the discovery of their life purpose. This journey begins with God.

If you want to emerge from the throes of problem driven life and find your purpose, you must seek God. When anybody wants to know the primary purpose, function or reason for something, the most obvious first step is to check with the manufacturer. The maker of something knows best why it was made, what it was made to do and how it best functions. You don't have to remain stuck on and in your problems. You can graduate to higher-level living.

III. WHAT IS PROMISE DRIVEN LIFE?

Promise driven people change the world. They challenge and change the climate. They alter the environment. They shift old and create new paradigms. They do old things in new ways. They do new and different things. They change the trajectory of human behavior. They modify and modulate the world's direction. They move the bar higher. They set new and higher standards.

Promise driven people change the world by first changing themselves. The change that promise driven people seek always impacts them first. **Promise driven people are the change they seek. Promise driven people are a picture of the world God wants.**

The world functions effectively when and where people know and live their purpose. **The world changes for the better when and where people live their promise.**

While achieving your purpose **can** have a worldwide impact, achieving your promise always has a worldwide impact. I dare to say most people don't see themselves as world citizens. But rather, see and define themselves based on some small, limited and parochial perspective that is substantially reduced from God's original Word/promise intention. Genesis 1:26 says, "Then God said, let us make man in our image, in our likeness, and let them rule over the fish of the sea and the birds of the air, over the livestock, over all the earth, and over all the creatures that move along the ground." This says to me that I have been 'made in the image and likeness of God...to rule...over all the earth.' I am here to impact the world. I am here to shape and reshape the world. I am here to be a world citizen, a citizen of the world. To think like a world citizen is at the beginning of promise driven life. **Small and limited thinking creates small and limited people who do small and limited things.**

Our material mind or self is always trying to re- duce things to their lowest common, manageable denominator. It is constantly constructing a restrictive, selective, self-centered, even selfish climate of least resistance. It seeks to limit inclusion of any potential trial, trouble, hardship or difficulty. Whereas our spiritual mind/self is always trying to include what would be the best for the most. This is the high road. This is the hard road. This is the road of promise that impacts the world.

Elijah took that road. As a promise driven person Elijah traveled God's path to promise. Elijah was a citizen of the world. He behaved in a way that was best for most. He spoke, believed and

34

behaved according to God's promise. He appears on the scene speaking God's truth/promise to Ahab the evil power of the country, Israel. Typical of promise driven people, he was not afraid to speak God's Word. And, he was not afraid to speak it to the existing and ruling powers. In 1 Kings 17:1 it is recorded that Elijah said to Ahab, "As the Lord God of Israel lives whom I serve, there will be neither dew nor rain in the next few years except at my word." This was bold behavior. This was daring behavior. This was promise driven behavior. Elijah was following God's path to promise. And though this path was the best for the most, it led directly to his life being endangered.

Elijah, one man, was accused by King Ahab of being solely responsible for all the trouble, drought, famine and subsequent starvation being experienced throughout the land. 1 Kings 18:16-17 says, "...so Ahab went to meet Elijah and said to him, Is that you, you troubler of Israel?" When you earn the designation of "troubler of Israel" you are having an impact that is far bigger and beyond yourself.

Paul also was a promise driven person. When he and Silas were in Thessalonica teaching and preaching, jealous Jews formed a mob to kill them. Acts 17:6-7 says, "But when they (the mob) did not find them they dragged Jason and some other brothers before the city officials, shouting: These men who have caused trouble all over the world have now come here and Jason has welcomed them into his house. They are all defying Caesar's

35

decrees, saying there is another king, one called Jesus."(NIV)   Paul and Silas were teaching and preaching a world-changing message, not just a life-changing message.   They were world citizens. Their message had worldwide impact.   And they were referred to as "these men who have caused trouble all over the world."   **Promise driven lives have impact that is far bigger, better and beyond themselves.**

Promise driven people (except for Jesus) are not perfect people, but they realize they serve a perfect God who does things perfectly.   As we align ourselves with and work towards achieving God's Word/promise,   our   lives   change,   we   solve problems, and we impact the world.

Promise driven life is lived based on and reaching for the promises of God.

Promise driven life is our greatest life possible.

Promise driven life is lived at its highest and best.

Promise driven life runs on all cylinders.

Promise driven life is fully and completely engaged in all aspects of living.

Promise driven life always challenges the status quo.

Promise driven life changes the atmosphere.

Promise driven life positively alters the environment.

Promise driven life is bigger, better and beyond purpose driven life. Though purpose driven life is good, blessed, and impactful, promise driven life is its maximation.

Promise driven life revolves around dreams, visions and imagination.

Promise driven life is one of peaceful pursuit. It is constantly stretching the envelope and reaching for "what can be".

Promise driven life is one of pursuit filled with the peace of knowing you are reaching for and doing the very best you can.

Promise driven life always impacts others.

Promise driven life is an instrument yielded to God. It demonstrates 'what is possible' or 'what can be'.

Promise driven life believes and behaves in the guarantee of God, the greatness of God and the goodness of God.

Promise driven life is always looking at and working towards the horizon versus looking at and working towards the bottom line. In fact for promise driven lives, the horizon is the bottom line.

Promise driven life is filled with the friction and frustration that accompany movement against the resistance of the status quo.

Promise driven life is always fighting for forward movement towards the highest possible numerator and against settling for the lowest common denominator.

Promise driven life takes the "high road". The high road is the hard road. The hard road is the road mentioned in Matthew 7:13-14 (NIV), "Enter through the narrow gate. For wide is the gate and broad is the road that leads to destruction and many enter through it. But small is the gate and narrow the road that leads to life, and only a few find it."

Promise driven life believes in and behaves consistent with the promises of God.

Promise driven life involves an activated individual with altruistic interests advancing God's initiatives of abundant increases.

Promise driven life is motivated by and aspires to mountaintops. It does not linger on or in the valleys.

A promise driven life displays mountaintop behavior even while in the valley. Mountaintop behavior is quite distinguishable from valley behavior, especially in the valley. Understanding and practicing valley behavior in the valley will serve the purpose of keeping you alive in the valley, and may even cause you to do well in the valley. But, you are still in the valley.

Promise driven life focuses on life's peaks rather than its pits.

Promise driven life performs at its peak though it may be in a pit.

Promise driven life exhibits peak performance even while in a pit.

Promise driven life understands that peak performances are most necessary in the pits of life.

Promise driven life constantly reaches for the highest and best.

Promise driven life focuses on results.

Promise driven life is outcome oriented.

Promise driven life is life that is empowered, enabled and emboldened.

Promise driven people continuously consider and are continuously consistent with promise in their spirit, speech and service.

People of promise periodically experience purging and pruning, sometimes on purpose and sometimes as an act of providence.

A promise driven person understands that every level of life has attitudes, beliefs and conduct that must be purged away in order to go to the next level.

Promise driven people change paradigms. They alter the atmosphere for the better. They change the way things are done.

Promise driven people are inspired by what's possible versus what's practical.

Promise driven people are pleasant even fun to be around, but very challenging.

Promise driven people live with conviction and challenge convention.

Promise driven people respond to a higher agenda, a higher calling, a God calling.

Promise driven people have higher thoughts and higher ways.

Promise driven people live liberated lives.

Promise driven people are life's heroes.

Promise driven people write their own story; one where they are the winner, versus letting someone else write one for them – where they are the loser.

Promise driven people are productive even during difficulty.

Promise driven people are absolutely clear about the source of their promise.

Promise driven people have a sense of calm and toughness in times of chaos and turmoil.

Promise driven people see and experience the divine during difficulty.

Promise driven people are productive in season and out of season.

Promise driven people stand out rather than fit in.

Promise driven people always have their better and best days in front of them.

Promise driven life always involves an activated individual with altruistic inclinations/ intentions to advance God's initiatives of abundant increases. In short, promise driven life has 4 elements:
1. an activated individual;
2. altruistic inclinations/intentions;
3. advancement of God's initiatives;
4. abundant increases.

Activated Individual

First of all, promise driven people are active and actively work on making something happen that is bigger, better and beyond themselves. Promise driven people are called activists. They are hard workers. They are smart workers. They are positive workers. They are energetic and enthusiastic workers. **The key is, promise driven people work.** They work like they know life depends on it. They work like they know work is the way to achieve God's promised Word/will/way. They actively work and work actively. Promise driven life requires an activated person. An activated person is one who is fired up. An activated person takes initiative, does, and gets things done. You don't find them hanging around waiting to be told what to do or, that something needs to be done. An activated person is always on the move mentally, physically and certainly, spiritually.

Activated people are known for not only being active, but for being actively involved in making things happen. Activated people are always busy. They always have something to do. Activated people are people who, if they were automobiles, would be filled up, started up and moving from place to place to do what needs to be done.

An activated individual is one who has received a revelation. Scripture makes clear the most activated people are those who have received a revelation. **Revelation is at the foundation of activation.** What is a revelation? It is a striking disclosure. It is God's disclosure to man of Himself and His will. It is an illogical but magnificent leap forward in awareness, knowledge and understanding of something. Revelation not only leads to, but causes activation. When you get a revelation about something you become activated around and about whatever it is. Spending significant time with God, being still, listening to and meditating on God's Word is an important part of the life of an activated individual. Stillness, undisturbed communion with God facilitates revelation from God. **Revelation is God in action. Revelation is God's method of activating or firing people up.** When God wants to activate an individual, He gives them a revelation. Sometimes it's a dramatic demonstration and other times it's a simple, soft whisper or feeling of being urged or nudged.

With Noah, it was a word from God that let him know that because of the condition of the world, he needed to take action to save himself and his family. Noah, a farmer, was activated in shipbuilding by a revelation from God. God simply spoke to Noah and said, "build an ark."(Genesis 6:14) Because of Noah's relationship with God, he knew God was talking to him, and therefore, he knew, with God's help, he could do what God was saying. Noah received a revelation from God, which inspired his activation in building an ark.

Activated individuals always stand out. They stand out because they work hard. They stand out because their work is excellent. They stand out because their work is different.

Abraham is another example of an activated individual. God spoke to him about how to achieve greatness or how to achieve God's promise. God told Abraham to 'get away from everything that was familiar, easy and comfortable' and 'travel to a place where everything is unfamiliar, challenging and uncomfortable'. To do this, he would have to follow God. And in doing this he would achieve the greatness of God's promise.(Genesis 12:1-3) Abraham's revelation sparked his activation on the most challenging journey of his life, the journey to promise. Some people get a revelation with or from a word from God. For others, God uses pictures.

Joseph had a dream. His dream came from God. His dream would not leave him alone. His dream was a revelation from God of things to come. Joseph's dream/revelation caused his activation toward its achievement. Once Joseph received his dream/revelation, things turned real sour in his life. However, his behavior remained consistent with the revelation God had given him. Joseph's journey was very long and very difficult. But because of his consistency and persistence, he succeeded in achieving God's promise. The story of Joseph is told in Genesis, chapters 37, and 39-50.

God used dreams to reveal Himself and His will to others as well. God gave Daniel a dream/revelation (Daniel 2:19, 28) that activated him to go and courageously speak to the king. God also gave Joseph, Jesus' earthly father, a dream/revelation that activated him to protect the baby Jesus.(Matthew 2:13-21)

In addition to words and dreams/visions/ pictures, God also uses dramatic demonstrations to get the attention of and reveal Himself to people. For example, Moses was on the backside of the desert in chapter three of the Book of Exodus when he noticed a bush that appeared to be on fire but was not being consumed. As the bush caught the attention of Moses, God spoke to him through the burning bush. God revealed to Moses the promised land set aside for His people, and that he was chosen to lead them to it. This revelation led to the activation of Moses as the leader of the people of Israel.

Paul also experienced a dramatic demonstration as God revealed Himself and His will. On the road to Damascus, Paul experienced a blinding light from heaven, which caused him to fall to the ground and hear the voice of Jesus speak to him. The revelation of God that came through the blinding light and voice, activated Paul on his journey to promise.(Acts 9)

The point of all this is, when God reveals to you Himself and His promise, you cannot help but become an activated individual. When you receive a word/promise/dream from God, it will not leave you alone. It will excite, inspire and motivate you. It will fill you up. It will fire you up. It will cause you to work at your highest and best to make it happen. When you get a revelation from God you will be activated. And if you are not activated, you have not yet received a revelation from God about who He is, who you are and what He has for you to do.

When an individual, a team, an organization, or a church get a revelation about their promise, they change. Their goals change. Their level of work changes. Their kind of work changes. Their intensity of energy, enthusiasm and effort changes.

Their attitude changes. Their interest and involvement change. Their level of faith and fight changes. They become new. They are transformed. Revelation is transforming. It changes who you are. It changes what you do. It changes how you do it. It changes what you say. It changes how you say it. **Revelation is the basis of activation.**

Altruisitic Intentions

The second element of a promise driven life is altruistic intentions. Altruism is unselfish concern for the welfare of others. Promise driven people are 'other' centered. God's promises are always altruistically inclined. They are always designed to touch the lives of others in a positive way. This is one of the best ways to determine that your promise/dream/vision is from God and not yourself. God always inspires in the direction of helping people. God's promise/dream/vision is usually directed outside of yourself. It is not only bigger, better and beyond where you are, it is this way for the specific purpose of reaching the most amount of others, and consequently, changing the world.

Self-centeredness and selfishness are not only disconcerting, they also disconnect. People who are self-centered and/or selfish cannot and will not achieve their promise. No matter how brilliant you are, you will not achieve your promise by always focusing on and trying to do your thing, your way for your reasons. Promise driven life is altruistic in nature. Promise driven people have an unselfish concern for the welfare of others. What are you working on that helps others? Who are you working with to better or improve them? How much time do you spend volunteering or giving of yourself to help a cause? Are you connected to any organization just to help? Are you active in your church? Do you live in a way that inspires and motivates others to do better or change? What are you committed to? Do your commitments involve other people or are they concentrated on you? What do you aspire to? Do your aspirations all focus on your needs, wants and desires? Answers to these questions will help you determine the level of altruism in your life, and thereby whether what you're passionate about comes from God or not. Remember, God blesses you to be a blessing.

Self-centered and selfish people block the flow of God's goodness in their lives. They block the manifestation of God's promise in their lives. God speaks to people and works through people. So, by definition, promise driven people must be altruistic. This is how God gets His agenda done.

The way to be more altruistic and break the pattern of self-centeredness and selfishness is to sow seeds of altruism. Be kind. Do random acts of kindness. Be kind when you don't feel like it. Be kind when you think you can't afford it. Be kind to self-centered and selfish people. **The way to see**

what you don't see is to be it. Another way to strengthen your altruism muscle is to volunteer at something. Volunteer at church. Volunteer in a specific ministry. Volunteer in a community-based organization. Volunteer at a local school. Volunteer at a local hospital. The key word here is, **volunteer.**

The essence of altruism is giving. You can strengthen your altruistic inclination by giving. John 3:16 says, "For God so loved the world that He gave His only son so that whoever believes in Him would not perish but have everlasting life." God is a giver. God is altruism. God's promise driven people are all altruistic. Love is unconditional acceptance. God loves us unconditionally. God accepts us unconditionally. God causes the sun to shine on people who do good and people who do bad. God is love. Love is mercy. Mercy is kindness. Kindness is altruism. Altruism characterizes promise driven life.

Advancing God's Initiatives

The third major element of a promise driven life is, the advancement of God's initiatives. What are God's initiatives? Simply put, God's initiatives are God's Word. Promise driven people are driven by the Word of God to initiate and establish the will and way of God. God's initiatives are efforts, directions, programs, projects and ministries that foster the spread of God's Word, will and way throughout the world. **We advance God's initiatives by living God's word.** We advance God's initiatives by living God's Word in all circumstances despite any difficulty. Promise driven lives advance God's initiatives because they are determined to live God's Word in good and bad times. They live God's Word when and where it's popular, and when and where it's not. They advance God's initiatives in the light and in the dark.

Promise driven people not only consistently advance God's program but also understand that they <u>are</u> God's program. Promise driven people understand that the advancement of God's Word/initiative not only begins with them, it is them. People advance God's program. People are God's program. Promise driven people know they are God's program. They are God's initiative. They know people will look at them and have their questions about God answered or have more questions about God raised. Promise driven people model their lives after God (Jesus) and practice the principles He teaches. They follow God and model Jesus.

Promise driven life is humble. Humility is necessary to advance God's initiatives. Humility is necessary because the tendency of man is toward the satisfaction of flesh. It is toward immediate gratification. It is toward self-centeredness and selfishness. Humility is controlled strength. It tracks closely with self-discipline. To advance God's initiatives and not your own, you must be able to deny self. Jesus said in Matthew 16:24, (NIV) "If any person will come after (follow) me, he must deny himself, pick up his cross and follow me." In other words, to advance God's initiatives, program, promise/dream/vision, you will have to be humble and disciplined.

Abundant Increase

The fourth major element of a promise driven life is abundant increase. Promise driven life is the most productive life. It is continuously and consistently productive. It is productive in good and smooth times. It is productive in bad and rough times. Jesus said in John 10:10(b), (NIV) "... I am come that you might have life in abundance." God's promise is always about abundance, more than enough, overflow. God's kingdom is a kingdom of abundance, more than enough, overflow. Ephesians 3:20 (NIV) says, "Now to him who is able to do immeasurably more than all we ask or imagine, according to his power that is at work within us." **God is all about abundance, overflow and more than**

enough. Promise driven lives are lives of abundance, overflow and more than enough.

Nature is a reflection of God's promise. Nature is a picture of abundance and increase. It is also a picture of abundant increase. Nature is the most productive entity known. And it all comes from God. The abundance of nature gives to us, sustains and prospers our life. Nature is a picture of God's promise to people who decide to live promise driven lives. All of the promise driven people in scripture lived lives of abundance and abundant increase. The list is long and varied and includes such as Job, Adam, Eve, Abraham, Sarah, Joseph, David, Abigail, Solomon, Isaac, Rebecca, Jacob, Rachel, Naomi, Ruth, Boaz, Moses, Joshua, Caleb, Mary, Martha, Lazarus, many disciples and Jesus.

Abundance, increase, overflow and more than enough, all describe the kingdom of God. They describe God's promise. They describe promise driven lives. **Abundant increase is the original intent of God for His people.** This is reflected in the Garden of Eden (Genesis 2:8-14), the promised land (Exodus 3:8-10), the Holy Spirit (Acts 2:1-12), and the new Jerusalem (Revelations 21:1-4). The thrust of the entire Bible is to move man to a place where abundance, increase, overflow, and more than enough are experienced. A promise driven life is what God wants for His people. Abundance, increase, overflow and more than enough are what promise driven people experience and accomplish. God's movement in scripture is always towards getting something to people. God is always trying to add to and multiply people. God's movement is always towards increase and more than enough.

Even in times of drought, famine and shortage, promise driven lives prosper. God blessed and prospered Isaac during and through a famine (Genesis 26:1-6). God blessed and prospered Egypt, Joseph's family and Joseph during and through the famine (Genesis 42:1-47:27). God blessed and prospered the poor and destitute widow of Zarephath during and through a famine (I Kings 17:1-16).

Promise driven people should expect to survive, even thrive during and through times of economic hardship. Promise driven people believe in and trust God as their source. Promise driven people, though out of a job, are never out of faith. Though they may temporarily have nothing in their hand, they have and hold God and His promise in their heart. When they have little to no material things or wealth, promise driven people still live lives of abundance, increase, more than enough and overflow. Promise driven people know and understand, you can always give kindness. You can always be kind to someone. You can be kind and give kindness like you are wealthy. Your circumstances should never dictate whether or not you are kind to others. Faith, love, mercy and kindness are heavenly currency that purchase for you far more than what you pay for. A promise driven life is an abundant life, rich in experience, challenge, struggle, trial, success, triumph, overcoming and change.

A promise driven life is a life of increase, where temporary shortages and shortfalls are not only just temporary, they are also periods of preparation for even greater increase. Promise driven life is a life where, by faith, there is always more than enough. Promise driven life is a life of overflow. Love overflows. Joy overflows. Peace overflows. Patience overflows. Righteousness overflows. Faith overflows. Humility overflows. Self-discipline overflows. Kindness overflows. It is a life where the fruit of God's spirit are in abundance. Promise driven life is a life of greatness. It is a life of service. The more you serve, the greater you'll be. The greater you are, the more blessed you'll be. The more blessed you are, the more you can serve. And the cycle continues around and around until you are living your greatest life possible, your life of promise where you are doing your very best to reach, touch and bless the most.

Promise driven life is a life lived for God, with God and by God.

IV. WHY LIVE PROMISE DRIVEN LIFE?

People want to win. They want to succeed. They want to be victorious. They want to achieve, accomplish and get things done. I believe this is built into us by our Creator. The desire to do something, to accomplish something, to be something of substance that makes a positive difference for yourself and others, is the way we're made. The most fundamental answer to the question, "Why live a promise driven life?" is because we were made to live one. The Bible says in Genesis 1:26, "And God said, let us make man in our image, after our likeness ... and let them have dominion ... over all the earth." We are made by the Creator. We are made by the Creator to be just like the Creator. **What God says is who God is. Who God is, is what God does.** This translates into a character of integrity, honesty and sincerity that stands on righteousness and peace. Promise is related to and involved in all these traits. At the core of promise are things like integrity, honesty, sincerity and righteousness. Promise cannot exist outside of these traits.

Why live a promise driven life? – because it is your best possible life. **Living a promise driven life will cause you to do**

your most to do your best. A promise driven life is your highest calling. A call from a city council person, mayor, governor, congressperson, senator or the president may be exciting and behavior changing. But, none of these compare to the call of God's promise/Word/dream/vision. God's promise is your highest calling and as such, should receive your most enthusiastic response.

Why live a promise driven life? Think about this. What kind of person makes a decision to remain crippled and confined to being carried rather than standing, walking and running on their own? What kind of person makes a decision to do little to nothing to improve things for themselves and their family rather than doing as much as they can to improve as much as they can? What kind of person decides to remain poor when they could prosper; to remain sick when they could be well; to remain ignorant when they could be informed and educated; to remain indifferent and apathetic when they could be loving and involved?

Why live a promise driven life? On a life scale of one to ten, a promise driven life is ten plus. What kind of person continues to live at level one and two when they could live at level ten? What is the character of someone who decides to take the low, and easy road of dependence on others rather than the high, hard road of self-discipline? What kind of person makes a decision to live like a caterpillar worm rather than a butterfly; to live as a seed rather than produce fruit and become an orchard; to live doing little rather than doing a lot; to live as a baby rather than become an adult; to live crying and complaining rather than growing up, assuming control and taking authority?

Why live a promise driven life? Because a promise driven person lives the most life possible. A promise driven person lives abundant life. They live and experience more love, joy, peace, patience, kindness, righteousness, faith, humility and self-discipline. They live and experience more of the essence of life. They have more challenges. And therefore, they have more opportunities for growth, development, maturity and enlargement. The path to promise is filled with gauntlets designed to prevent change and keep things the same. Promise driven people take this path, face and defeat the gauntlets, and succeed. They succeed in establishing a new standard. They succeed in restructuring the status quo. They succeed in breaking out of the orbit of ordinariness and routineness. They succeed in breaking through the gravitational pull of "this is the way things are done" and "there is no way you can change and do better."

Why live a promise driven life? Because people who live promise driven lives experience more excitement. What can be more exciting than facing the big challenges in your life standing between you and your promise? What is more exciting than working on changing the way things are done based on what you bring into existence? What can be more exciting than inventing something that you know will help many people successfully grapple with their Goliath? What is more exciting than succeeding at being the best you can be? What can be more exciting than overcoming an opposition hurdle that, in the past, kept you from making the kind of progress that puts you closer to your promise? What is more exciting than knowing the giant negatives in your life can fall, and watching them come down?

Why live a promise driven life? You'll have more fun. To follow the path of promise is to practice its principles. To practice the principles (steps to promise) of promise is to achieve the promise. It's a guarantee. Knowing you will achieve promise puts a smile on your face even through serious adversity. I believe this is what scripture refers to when it says in Psalm 22:3 that 'God inhabits the praise of His people.' I believe the message here is God, who is His Word/promise lives in His peoples' obedience to His Word/promise. In other words, people who live by consistently practicing the principles of promise never hesitate to experience the joy of the reality of God's promise before and while it is being fully manifested.

A good example of this is the experience of Paul and Silas in the sixteenth chapter of Acts. They were beaten and put in jail. Though they were imprisoned, they still pursued God's promise. They were promise driven people. Though in prison they nevertheless remained driven by God's promise. They decided to shape and reshape their circumstances. They took control of and authority over their environment. They made a decision to make the best of a bad situation. They decided to experience what they would experience if they were free, though they were imprisoned. 'They sang praises to God' loud enough for the other prisoners to hear and be impacted. They lived the principles of God's promise while locked in a prison. They did not allow being in prison to make them decide to live like a prisoner. **Living like a prisoner keeps you in prison. It keeps you locked up and limited. It keeps you living beneath your privilege and certainly below your promise.**

Deciding to live a promise driven life frees your spirit to continue pursuing the Word/promise though your body may be restricted in its movement. When your spirit is free and focused on God's Word/promise/vision for your life, your body will be not too far behind. The promise driven lives of Paul and Silas not only broke their chains, but the chains of the other prisoners as well. The promise driven lives of Paul and Silas not only opened their doors, but the doors of the other prisoners as well.

Why live a promise driven life? Promise driven life is always bigger, better and beyond you.

It not only impacts you, but others as well. In fact, a case could be made for the fact that Paul and Silas were imprisoned for the purpose of exposing the prisoners to promise driven life. And thereby, the prisoners would be freed and afforded the opportunity to decide to be promise driven people versus problem driven people.

Why live a promise driven life? Because promise driven people break chains and open doors. They loose and liberate. They untie and let go. They lift and lead. They inform and inspire. They give help and hope. They give their time, temple (body), talent and treasure to making the world a better place beginning with themselves.

I want to provide my attempt at a contrast comparison between problem driven, purpose driven and promise driven life. Hopefully, this will provide a context to make what comes next more understandable, and thereby, facilitate a decision to avoid problem driven life and transition from a life of purpose to a life of promise.

A LIFE DRIVEN BY:

PROBLEMS	PURPOSE	PROMISE
comes from man	comes from God	comes from God
not knowing and not caring why I'm here: ignorance and apathy	knowing why I'm here	knowing what is possible because I'm here
stagnant	static in nature That is, once purpose is achieved, there's a tendency towards complacency and satisfaction at this level of living.	dynamic in nature It is a continuous quest for your highest and best.
no commitment	commitment to being a tree that bears fruit	commitment to being an orchard
no change	change self	change the world
lazy	energy	enthusiasm
unprepared to be in the game	to be in the game	to be a champion
existence	life	abundant life
weakness	strength	strength and courage
lackadaisical	persistence	persistence and boldness
selfish/ self-righteous	self-oriented self-reliant	selfless
emptiness	meaning	meaning/vision/ imagination

A LIFE DRIVEN BY:

PROBLEMS	PURPOSE	PROMISE
resentful	meaningful	meaningful and joyful
no goals	goals and objectives	dreams
scattered, no focus	focus: the bottom line	focus: the horizon
low level living	good level living	highest level living
not getting in the boat	getting in the boat to cross the lake	getting out of the boat and walking on water
Barack Obama in business	Barack Obama in politics	Barack Obama as President of the United States of America
poor/averageness	good/goodness	great/greatness
blames others	assumes responsibilities	takes authority over circumstances
focus: me, mine, my	focus: me and how I fit with others	focus: me and what I can do to help others
procrastinates	responsive	takes initiative
dependent	independent	interdependent
complaints/cowardice	concerns/cooperation	courage/ connection
condemning	conserving	constructing

A LIFE DRIVEN BY:

PROBLEMS	PURPOSE	PROMISE
contentious (always against something)	caring (protective of what is)	composing/ creating (bringing into existence something new)
tearing down	maintaining	building and rebuilding
excuses	reasons	affirmations
ignorance/illiteracy	information/ knowledge	education/wisdom
slavery	freedom	full potential/ promise/liberation
negative attitude	positive attitude	optimistic/ enthusiastic attitude
negative and inactive	positive and active	optimistic and enthusiastically active
wants what others have	wants their own	wants to help others get their own
constantly critical	gives constructive comments	commends and blesses others
below average and average performance	good and very good performance	excellent and magnificent performance
stingy and cheap	meets obligation/duty	generous and giving
wants relief to feel better	wants respect and tries to do better	seeks revelation and transformation to be better

Jesus is the best example of promise driven life. He talked about it in different ways at different times. In John 6:35 Jesus said, "I am **the** bread of life. He who comes to me will never go hungry and he who believes in me will never be thirsty." In verse 51 Jesus says, "I am **the** living bread that came down from heaven. If anyone eats this bread, he will live forever."

In other words Jesus is saying, "There is nothing better for you than what I am offering. There is nothing higher for you than what I am offering. There is nothing greater for you than what I am offering. In other words, what I am offering you, if accepted, will cause you to reach your most, best and highest. You will reach your promise."

Jesus said on another occasion in John 8:12 (NIV), "I am **the** light of the world. Whoever follows me will never walk in darkness, but will have the light of life." In other words, Jesus says model me and you will always walk in a path towards goodness and blessing no matter how bad and dark the surrounding circumstances may be. When you model Jesus you continue on the path of your promise (your most, highest and best), despite the presence of many problems.

Further, Jesus says in John 10:9, "I am **the** door; whoever enters through me will be saved. He will come in and go out, **and** find pasture." His next statement adds to this with these words, "...I have come that they may have life, and have it to the full."(NIV) The idea here is, Jesus is all about life in abundance, life overflowing. **Abundant life and overflowing life is a promise driven life.** And so, modeling Jesus is "the door" to a life of abundance and overflow. **Abundance and overflow characterize God's promises.**

Abundance and overflow are the characteristics of the Garden of Eden in Genesis 2:8-9 where it says, "God planted a garden toward the east, in Eden (delight); and there He put the man whom He had formed ... and out of the ground God made grow every tree that is pleasant to the sight or to be desired – good for food; the tree of life also in the center of the garden and the tree of the knowledge of (the difference between) good and evil and blessing and calamity."(Amplified Version, AV)

Abundance and overflow also characterize the "promised land" mentioned in Exodus 3:8 where God speaks to Moses by saying, "I have come down to deliver them out of the hand and power of the Egyptians and to bring them up out of that land to a land good and large, a land flowing with milk and honey (a land of plenty) – to the place of the Caananite, Hittite, Amorite, Perrizite, Hivite and Jebusite." (AV)

Abundance and overflow are characteristics of the Holy Spirit as well. Where and when the spirit of God moves in scripture, what happens is not only great and awesome, but also everybody connected is impacted. For example, in the beginning in Genesis 1:2 it says, "The earth was without form and an empty waste and darkness was upon the face of the deep. The spirit of God was moving (hovering, brooding) over the face of the waters."(AV) Once the spirit of God moved, God spoke. When God's spirit was moved, He spoke into existence what was in His spirit. The spirit of God is always moved in the direction of order, organization, structure or life. The spirit of God moved, God spoke and there emerged the abundance and overflow of the universe, earth, our world and nature. In Acts 2:24 the abundance and overflow of the spirit of God is further detailed by this description, "when suddenly there came a sound from heaven like the rushing of a violent tempest blast, and it **filled** the **whole** house in which they were sitting … and there appeared to them tongues resembling fire… which settled on **each** one of them. And they were **all** filled (diffused throughout their souls) with the Holy Spirit and began to speak in other (different, foreign) languages (tongues) as the spirit kept giving them clear and loud expression (in each tongue, in appropriate words)."(AV) The Holy Spirit was a promise given by God through Jesus. In Luke 24:49 Jesus says, "I will send forth upon you what my Father has promised; but remain in Jerusalem until you are clothed with power from on high." Acts1:8 says, "You shall receive power (ability, efficiency, and might) when the Holy Spirit comes upon you and you shall be my witnesses in Jerusalem and all Judea and Samaria and to the ends (the very bounds) of the earth."(AV)   What this means to me is **the spirit of God, which is the promise of God, brings the power of God to achieve the promises of God for the people of God.**

A 'witness' for God is 'evidence' for God. And **the best evidence for God are people walking in the promise of God.** And **the promise of God is abundance and overflow for the individual, with a design to impact others.   Remember, your promise (dream or vision) comes to you from God, but it is never just for you.**

This point is further made by what happened in the disciples after receiving and yielding to the Holy Spirit.   **First, they were generally empowered.**   They started experiencing dominion and authority over their circumstances and situations.   And they began to take charge of their life direction.   It is at this time that the disciples – who were already followers of Jesus The Christ – developed the **mindset of maximization.**   They now were walking in the promise of God – to reach everybody, everywhere – which is the maximization of their purpose, originally stated by Jesus as being transformed from fishermen to 'fishers of men'. They had now been elevated to their highest road, as they responded to their highest calling (promise) and were headed for their greatest impact.

Second, the disciples were enabled. They received and developed the gift of talent and skill in language, giving them the ability to communicate with people far beyond their immediate race, culture and ethnicity. This gift blessed them by expanding their reach and enlarging their territory. Now instead of being a fisher of men only in the area of Galilee, they were enabled to fish for men everywhere in the known world.

Third, the disciples were emboldened. They became more bold and daring. Purpose can be achieved through the normal but persistent pursuit of life's most basic questions like, "Why am I here? What am I supposed to be doing? And, what is the point of life?" **Promise on the other hand, requires boldness and daring.** Promise requires some bravery and audacity. **The spirit of God pushes you towards the promise of God.**

When Peter and John were arrested for preaching about Jesus' resurrection, it was clear that these men were now driven by the promise of God in and on their lives. In their trial, when asked, "By what power or authority did you minister this miracle?" Acts 4:8-10 says, Peter (because he was filled with and controlled by the Holy Spirit, said to them, ... "It is in the name and through the power and authority of Jesus Christ ... whom you crucified, but whom God raised from the dead, in Him and by means of Him this man is standing here before you well and sound in body."(AV) Because of the presence of God's promise (Holy Spirit) in their lives they were now promise driven people. And they were now living promise driven lives. The disciples were no longer backing down or backing away from the path to promise. They were strong, courageous, daring and bold in prosecuting their case. And people noticed and were impacted by the difference.

Acts 4:13 says when they (rulers and members of Sanhedrin Council) saw the boldness and unfettered eloquence of Peter and John and perceived that they were unlearned and untrained in the schools (common men with no educational advantages) they marveled; and they recognized that they had been with Jesus. Further, after being warned, threatened and forbidden to teach at all in or about the name of Jesus, they defied the warnings, threats and demands and "continued to speak the Word of God with freedom and boldness and courage." The disciples, emboldened by the presence and control of the promise of the spirit of God, had decided and were now determined to live a promise driven life. And the results of this decision were the same as they always are for promise driven people, abundance and overflow.

Acts 4:33 says, "With great strength and ability and power the apostles delivered their testimony to the resurrection of the Lord Jesus, and great grace (loving-kindness and favor and goodwill) rested richly upon them all."(AV)

V. HOW TO DISCOVER/UNCOVER YOUR PROMISE

1) What difference do you make?

You were born to make a difference. I was born to make a difference. We are here to make a difference. What difference do I make? What difference do you make? Do I make a difference? Do you make a difference? What difference are you suppose to make? What difference am I supposed to make? How do I uncover it? How will I know it? How do I know I'm supposed to make a difference? This prescription, 'From Purpose to Promise Driven Life: A Prescription for Making the Difference You Were Born to Make,' explores and provides responses to these questions and others. It is designed to inform, inspire and motivate you toward your God-given promise, which is the means by which you will make the difference you were born to make.

Often I have found myself wondering about the purpose or point of certain creatures. Included in my thoughts are, what difference do certain creatures make? I've wondered, what is the point of a centipede, a mosquito or a hippopotamus? What do they do to make a difference on the planet?

71

What is their contribution to ecological stability or advancement? Why does the earth need anteaters? Or termites? If God made ants, why did He make another creature to eat them? If God made trees of wood, why did He make another creature that eats wood?

A brief examination of the life sustaining, ecological balance of nature makes it clear that all creatures are here to make a difference. And, the difference they make is quite impactful. Consider the bat. Many look at the bat and see nothing more than a flying rat. According to the New World Encyclopedia, "a small, brown bat can consume up to 600 mosquitoes an hour. They also are effective at removing agricultural pests. In one agricultural season, a typical colony of about 150 big, brown bats in the Midwest eats 50,000 leafhoppers, 38,000 cucumber beetles, 16,000 Junebugs, 19,000 stink bugs and thousands of moths, cornborers, earthworms and cutworms." Beetles, bugs, hoppers and worms destroy crops. They can negatively impact our food supply in a big way. So, they must be held in balance. Brown bats help maintain the insect balance that preserves our crops from destruction and fosters our food supply. Bats, especially in combination with birds, make a big difference in controlling the insect population and thereby make a positive difference for our food supply.

All life forms are here to make a difference that enhances life on planet earth. If that difference is not made, an imbalance of life occurs. This imbalance may take the form of extinction of a species, an over supply of crop predators leading to the destruction of certain crops, limited food supply and significant food shortages in certain geographical areas, economic hardship for large segments of the agriculture industry, or a combination of all of the above.

To make a difference is to have an effect, to make an impact, to change the situation, or to alter the environment. Promise driven people make a difference. They alter the environment. They change the situation. Promise driven people are difference makers. They are game changers. They are paradigm shifters and envelope stretchers. People care about the presence or absence of a promise driven person, and at a minimum, know when they are missing. Promise driven people are missed because they make a difference. They have an impact. They change the situation.

A good example of one person making a difference in another's life is the impact made by Naomi on Ruth. Naomi, her husband and two sons, left Bethlehem where they were experiencing extremely hard times. There was a famine. Over a ten-year period, Naomi's husband and their two sons died leaving Naomi and her two daughters-in-law, widows. Naomi decided to go back home and pleaded with her daughters-in-law to go back to their own families. One of them agreed and left to return home. The other, Ruth, was so impacted by

Naomi that she said in Ruth 1:16 (NIV), "Don't urge me to leave you or to turn back from you. Where you go I will go, and where you stay I will stay. Your people will be my people and your God will be my God. Where you die, I will die, and there I will be buried. May the Lord deal with me ever so severely if anything but death separates you and me." Naomi made a difference in the life of Ruth. Naomi changed Ruth's life. The book of Ruth is really the story of Naomi. Naomi lived a promised driven life. She spent the latter part of her life focused on mentoring, growing, developing, protecting and prospering Ruth. And even before this time, Naomi so lived before Ruth that Ruth refused to return home to her own family but remained with Naomi.

At the foundation of promise driven life is the desire to make a positive difference for others. Naomi's impact on Ruth is not the only example in scripture. There are others. Abraham made a difference for Lot. Joseph made a difference for his family. Moses made a difference for the people of Israel. David made a difference for King Saul and the people of Israel. Paul made a difference in the life of Timothy, Titus and the growth and development of the early church. Jesus made a difference in every life He touched.

What difference do you make? What difference can you make? What difference are you supposed to make? **Promise driven people make a difference in the lives of others.** This is because promise driven people are difference makers, game changers, paradigm shifters, envelope stretchers, visionaries and revolutionaries. Promise driven people are so concerned about others their lives are distinguished by the positive impact they seem to always have. Difficult circumstances, hard times, hard tasks, hard trials or trouble never keep promise driven people from positively impacting peoples' lives.

The difference you can and do make in the lives of others is related to your God-given gifts. It is my belief that everybody on earth is gifted in some way. The area of your gift is the area of your greatest impact. It is also the area where your promise/dream/vision will most likely come from.

For example, David was a poet/warrior/leader. His anointing was to be king. David's highest potential, his promise was to be a great king/leader of men. From the time his promise of being king was revealed to him, he began to behave in a kingly manner. He began to make king-type and king-sized differences in the lives of people with whom he made contact. While an outlaw, running for his life from King Saul and hiding in a cave, David, a promise driven person, became king over hundreds of men who were characterized by and driven by the problems of being in debt, in distress and discontented. These men, living problem driven lives, found their way to David who was hiding and living in a cave.

1 Samuel 22:1-2 says, "David escaped to the cave of Adullam ... All those who were in distress or in debt or discontented gathered around him, and he became their leader. About four hundred men were with him." He became their leader despite the fact he was running for his life and hiding from the king. He became such a leader and made such an impact on the lives of these men that they were transformed from men of debt, distress and discontent to "mighty men". David accomplished this while **his** life was going through the valley of the shadow of death. He did not allow what he was going through to keep him from exercising his gifts and living his promise. **Gifts and promise are connected.**

Both Joseph and Daniel were gifted in the area of "dream interpretation". Both of them were afforded opportunities and used their gifts to achieve their promise. Their gifts made room for them. They had faith in and used the gifts God gave them to achieve God's promise for their lives.

What is your gift? What makes you stand out? What are you very good at? What do others positively comment on about you? What do others frequently request of you? What do your parents, elders or others who know and have known you, say you are good at? What brings you joy when you do it or talk about it? Answers to these questions and others like them will help you discover what your gift is and thereby, what differentiates you, and thereby, what difference you are here to make, and thereby, the area where your greatest potential or promise lies.

You were born to make a difference. You can make that difference only by being a participant in life. The difference you make is most likely to be in the area of your gift. **Your gift can be discovered by exploring the intersection between what brings you joy, what you are good at, get good results from and enjoy doing, and what others give you frequent compliments about.**

When you are willing to make the difference you are here to make, you earn your seat at the table of promise. God sits at the head and parcels out His promise to those willing to step up to the table. Your seat at the table of promise is earned. All are welcome, but your seat must be earned. And your seat is earned by making a difference such that when you are absent, not only do people notice, they care, and are concerned.

Do people care or even notice that you are absent from work? Family? Church? Ministry? Business? The team? You are missed when you have earned your seat/space/place in the life of your relationship, family, church, ministry, business or organization. Being missed means more than people just knowing your name. A famous name is notoriety. It means your name has been mentioned often for some reason. Adolph Hitler has a famous name. Charles Manson has a famous name. Jeffrey Dahmer, Willie Lynch, Bull O'Connor and Osama Bin Laden all have famous names but are not missed. We know the names of heart disease, cancer, stroke, diabetes, rheumatoid arthritis, multiple sclerosis and obesity as well. But, we don't miss them when they are not around.

So, when Jonathan said to David in 1 Samuel 20:18, "Tomorrow is the new moon festival. You will be missed, because your seat will be empty," he was referring not only to his normal chair but also, the place David had earned in his heart and the hearts of others. **You are missed when you have earned a place in peoples' hearts.** You earn space in peoples' hearts when you make a difference for them. You make a difference for people through acts of kindness, grace, mercy, strength, boldness and daring.

In your church or ministry you have to earn your "seat". You are not missed because you are a member. **You cannot be missed if no one knew you were present in the first place.** You are missed when you make a difference in the life and wellbeing of the church/ministry. You have to earn your "seat" in your company or on your team. Otherwise, you are not missed. Championship teams, organizations, businesses, churches, and relationships have people who are intensely serious about earning their place in the life of the collective effort to achieve their goal.

Generally people are most willing to work hard at something they enjoy doing. People are enthusiastic about working, making a difference and 'earning their seat' when they are doing things they enjoy. Your gift is at the intersection of what you are good at, and what you enjoy doing. With the help of concerned others you can look over your past and present life to discover that intersection. When you find the intersection, affirm it. Declare to yourself that 'this' is who you are. Talk about it with others. Think about it yourself. Reflect on it. Refine it. Research it.

At different times, on different occasions, in different ways, to different people, Jesus repeatedly said and affirmed He was the Son of God. And, His mission was to show humanity the way to abundant life here on earth and eternal life with God. Jesus was clear about where His intersection was. Jesus knew His joy intersected with being obedient to God's Word. This was therefore His gift. This was the difference Jesus came to make. Jesus was uniquely gifted to make the difference of showing humanity how to live obedient to God's Word. As Jesus was God in the flesh, He was good at living God's Word. And, in addition to being good at it, He enjoyed doing it. So, at the intersection of Jesus' joy and what He was good at, was His gift, 'obedience to the Word of God'.

In John 15:9-12 Jesus says, "As the Father has loved me so have I loved you. Now remain in my love. If you obey my commands you will remain in my love, just as I have obeyed my Father's commands and remain in His love. I have told you this so that my joy may be in you and that your joy may be complete. My command is this: Love each other as I have loved you."(NIV)

Jesus was so good at being obedient to God's Word and while doing it His joy was so great, that's all He did. Jesus was all consumed by His gift. Jesus was His gift. Jesus was "The Word" of God. When you are fortunate enough to discover your gift area and are able to earn a living working in it, you will be your most enthusiastic, energetic, committed, persistent and determined self. You will be living your promise.

President Obama is good at and enjoys capturing abstract concepts like democracy, unity, legacy, prosperity, cooperation, and community and translating them into an inspirational, common vision for large numbers of people. He knows where the intersection is of what he's good at and what he enjoys doing. He knows his gift. He's giving it. He's living at the level of promise.

Martin Luther King, Jr. was masterful at packaging and presenting to America the contradictions existing between its principles and practices. And, he enjoyed his work. He was aware of the intersection of what he was good at and what he enjoyed doing. He knew his gift. He lived his life at the level of promise.

George Washington Carver was one of the world's greatest scientists. On his gravestone at Tuskeegee Institute in Tuskeegee, Alabama, is inscribed, "He could have added fortune to fame, but caring for neither he found happiness and honor in being helpful to the world." George W. Carver was a world citizen who made a worldwide impact by making the difference he was born to make. He knew what his gift was. He knew where the intersection was between what he was good at and what he enjoyed doing. His work (according to Wikipedia Encyclopedia) resulted in the creation of 325 products from peanuts, more than 100 products from sweet potatoes and hundreds more from a dozen other plants. He lived his life at the level of promise.

2) Roller Coaster Attitude

It is interesting to note that the roller coaster is often the most popular ride at the amusement park. It has long lines of people seeking to get on, get strapped in and take off. In fact, according to the website, ultimate rollercoaster.com, roller coasters are the world's most popular amusement park ride. This website says further, "Roller coasters have been a 'must ride' attraction at amusement and theme parks for more than a century."

Roller coasters are designed to be the biggest, highest, fastest, wildest, scariest, most intimidating ride at the amusement park. This point is supported by the names, sizes, heights, speeds and courses of roller coasters. They have names like: Kingda Ka, Steel Dragon, Goliath, Millennium Force, Titan, Desperado, Phantom's Revenge, Son of Beast, El Toro, Mean Streak, Cyclone, Collossus, Tower of Terror, Mr. Freeze, Wicked Twister, and the Chiller. They have heights of over 400 feet (equivalent to a thirty to forty story building), reach speeds of over 120 mph, cover distances of over 8,000 feet, make twists, turns, loops, and cause people to scream because of the adrenalin generating, fear-filled, but thoroughly thrilling experience.

Despite the height, speed, twists, turns and loops, they are the most popular rides. Despite the fear and terror-inducing names they are still the most sought after ride experience at the amusement park. In fact, many would say it is **because** of the height, distance, speed, twists, turns, and loops that people seek out and ride roller coasters. This is borne out by the fact that the trend in roller coasters, since their inception in the early 1900's, has been always in the direction of being bigger, taller, faster, scarier with more and sharper twists, turns and loops.

One amusement park, Cedar Point in Sandusky, Ohio, is known as the roller coaster capital of the world, and has at this time, 17 roller coasters out of a number of rides that total at least 70. And, according to the website, roller-coaster.com, the 17 roller coasters (22-24% of the total available rides) are responsible for close to 50% of the ride experiences at the park.

Why do people, seemingly instinctively, seek out the biggest, wildest, fastest, loopiest, scariest, most twisted, convoluted, fear-inducing and scream-causing experience at amusement parks? Could it be that there is something in people that makes us desire being excited, deeply moved, intensely stirred, simultaneously fearful and joyful? Could it be that life lived at its peak brings into play the extremes of emotional intensity? Could it be that despite the gravitational pull of the ordinary and safe, there is something in us constantly reaching for highest-level living?

Roller coasters are often described as thrilling. They are designed for thrill seekers. What is a thrill? I think a thrill is an experience that reaches and touches deep inside you with emotional intensity. A thrill results from the combined impact of intense emotions, especially from opposite directions. A thrill results from the combined presence of intense exhilaration and apprehension. It is the simultaneous occurrence of uncertainty, fear, achievement and excitement. The experience of a thrill can be described as the fear inherent in uncertainty of outcome co-existing with the excitement of achieving something new and unusual. Looked at another way, a thrill can be understood as the feeling of excitement that comes from facing the fear of uncertainty of outcome while meeting the challenge of doing something new and different. More simply put, it is the excitement of facing the fear, uncertainty and doubt of new discovery, new territory, new direction and meeting the challenge.

We seek the thrill of victory in life. However, like the roller coaster, the thrills are inherent in being bigger, higher, faster, scarier and more intimidating with greater twists, turns and loops.

The roller coaster can be a metaphor for life. It starts with a decision to get on. At first, things go very slow; there is the long waiting period in line -- this reflects your commitment and accountability to your decision. Then there is choosing your seat location, getting on board, and being securely strapped in -- this reflects your preparation and maturity for your new adventure. Then things begin to happen. The movement begins. It's an uphill journey. The going is slow, and difficult. The climb is high and steep. But eventually, the top is reached and the speed at which things occur changes drastically -- this is analogous to life's steps toward and to productivity.

Then, after the achievement of high speeds, there come twists, curves, turns, single, double and triple loops, all accompanied by extremely loud, long and strong screams indicating the simultaneous presence of intense exhilaration and apprehension.

In life refinement (purging, pruning) can be quite difficult. The process of refinement, stretches, strengthens, changes, purifies, transforms, expands, enhances and enlarges you.

The curves, turns, twists and loops that life presents can be devastating. They can derail us. They can turn us over. They can throw us for a loop. They can turn us upside down. Especially since they are entered into at the speed of life with no time to stop, get off, and think before you proceed. In life, we spend a fair amount of energy trying to avoid or minimize it's high, steep climbs, its fast and ferocious declines, its curves, turns, twists and loops. In fact, in life, any course of activity that is widely accepted as being very difficult usually has a short line. But, despite the high and steep climbs, the fast and furious drops, the many curves, turns, twists and loops with roller coasters, people seek them out, get in line and ride.

In life, the people who seek and maximize such experiences are driven by promise. The people who get on and seek to minimize the climbs, curves, turns and twists, I see as driven by purpose. And the people who seek to altogether avoid the high climbs, deep drops, curves, turns, twists and loops are driven by problems.

Promise driven people approach life like roller coaster lovers approach roller coasters. They love life at its fullest potential, in its most positive direction having its greatest impact. They love life at full throttle. They love life at its highest, fastest,

85

steepest, curviest and most challenging. Promise driven people get in the line for the toughest opponent, hardest task, and biggest challenge. They understand this is where the greatest effect is, and the greatest results can be achieved.

The greatest moments in temporal human history are those that intersect with the eternal divinity. These moments tend to be filled with great apprehension and exhilaration. Scriptural examples include the set of events surrounding the birth and death of Jesus. Luke 2:8-20 describes the birth of Jesus from the perspective of shepherds living nearby. The shepherds were terrified at the appearance of an angel who brought the best news humans have ever received.

The moment was filled with the thrill of the combined presence of apprehension at the angelic appearance and exhilaration with the expression of the good news of great joy. The lives of the shepherds were so impacted by their intersection with the eternal divinity, they returned "glorifying and praising God."

The experience of the shepherds could be seen from another perspective. Whenever people receive a revelation about their true promise, their life behavior changes to be consistent with that promise (Jesus), they become a 'new creature'. They are infused with new DNA that is consistent with new birth. This new DNA is a **d**ivine, **n**ew **a**genda. It is divine because promise/dream/vision comes from

God. It represents all you are here to accomplish. It is new because it is a different perspective on life and a different way of living. And of course, the agenda (things to be done) flows from the new and different promise/dream/vision that now drives your life.

Another intersection of temporal human history with eternal divinity occurred at the resurrection.

Mary Magdalene and other women were on their way to the grave of Jesus wondering how they could remove the large stone impediment covering the opening of His grave. Matthew 28:2-8 says, "There was a violent earthquake for an angel of the Lord came down from heaven and, going to the tomb, rolled back the stone and sat on it." v.5, The angel said to the women, "Do not be afraid for I know you are looking for Jesus who was crucified." v.6, "He is not here, he has risen just as He said." v.7, "Go quickly and tell His disciples. He has risen from the dead..." v.8, "The women hurried away from the tomb afraid, yet filled with joy....."(NIV). Once again, we have here the thrilling, simultaneous presence of great fear and great joy, of intense apprehension and intense exhilaration.

This passage of scripture could be viewed from another vantage point. Earth is always shaken up and shaken loose when visited by heaven. When you get a revelation about your true promise it shakes you up and wakes you up to the different and new you with new concepts, conversation and conduct. When you understand and appreciate that

God's guaranteed promise/dream/vision for you unveils **all** you are here to accomplish, you should be inspired, encouraged and enabled in behavior that is steadfast and consistent with it. When you get a revelation about your highest potential, your promise/dream/vision, it shakes you loose from the shackles of devaluing concepts, discouraging conversation and destructive conduct.

If life were an amusement park, promise driven people would all be on or in the lines for the roller coaster. The roller coaster is the biggest, tallest, steepest, fastest, curviest, most twisted, most looped, most intimidating ride experience in the park. More than all other rides, it is most likely to have the greatest impact on you and to be the topic of discussion concerning your visit to the amusement park.

Purpose driven people would be satisfied with being in the park and having access to the roller coaster and perhaps occasionally getting on.

Problem driven people would be outside blaming someone for why they could not gain admission to the park. And, if and when they do gain admission, most or much of their time would be spent making excuses about why they don't go near the roller coaster. They would say things like, "It's too big;" "It goes too high;" "It moves too fast;" "The turns are too sharp;" "I don't want to be thrown for a loop;" "What if I fall off?"

Promise driven people live their lives based on all they can be. Their promise/dream/vision is at the center of their life. Decisions, reactions, responses are all made with a focus on their promise. So that even when traveling through the valley of the shadow of death or delayed for a while in the valley of dry bones, promise driven people continue to reflect their promise. So, they do not engage in discouraging conversation or destructive conduct, nor do they suddenly switch and allow devaluing concepts to determine their decisions and directions.

While in the valleys and when headed to a valley, like people on a roller coaster, they may cry and scream loud and a lot. But they know they are just passing through and will soon be headed back up. This is why promise driven people are always positive and helpful to others wherever they are and in whatever they are going through. Because they know, to behave otherwise is to be distracted and detoured. Promise driven people, like everybody else, feel fear, but unlike everybody else, continue to move forward. For them the joy and exhilaration associated with determination to reach the destination outweigh the fear and apprehension associated with the difficulty of the journey.

What do you have a roller coaster lover's attitude about? About what habit or hobby do you have a roller coaster lover's attitude? Is there an area in your life or some thing you love doing or talking about so much that you have a roller coaster lover's attitude about it? Answers to these questions and others like them will help you discover your promise. What recurring dream do you have that despite the difficulty of its achievement, still excites, exhilarates and invigorates you when you talk about it?

A very important characteristic of promise driven people that also distinguishes roller coaster lovers is, they enjoy the journey. The reason roller coasters are continually being made higher, faster, curvier, steeper, more twisted, with more turns and loops is, the ride is key. There is a primary focus on the ride/journey. The more turns, twists and loops there are, the better. The higher and steeper it is, the better. The faster it is, the better. For the roller coaster lover the ride is the thing. Handling the ride is "making **it** happen."

The joy for the roller coaster lover is not as much in finishing the ride as it is in the ride itself.

Likewise, promise driven people understand there is joy in the journey. It is not something you arrive at so you can sit down and settle in. A promise driven singer is one who is excited about the journey to being a Grammy, award-winning singer. A promise driven athlete is excited about the journey to being a world champion athlete. A promise driven businessperson is excited about the journey to being a multibillion dollar business owner. A promise driven principal is excited about the journey to being the best school on earth. A promise driven politician is excited about the journey to being the best politician possible at the highest level of politics. A promise driven church is excited about the journey to being "the best church on earth." A promise driven ministry is excited about the journey to being a world-class ministry with worldwide impact.

Notice there are some things in life which have long, difficult, and often dangerous journeys attached to them but, the possibility of their achievement is still exciting and exhilarating. An important part of discovering your promise/dream/vision is identifying what those things are, or what that thing is for you.

Promise driven people are journey-oriented. They know life and promise are a journey. They know the journey can be long, difficult and even dangerous. But, they also know there is joy in the journey. And the joy in the journey inspires continuous progress.

What brings you joy? What brings you joy no matter what the circumstances are in which you experience it? What causes your heart to smile? What makes you smile on the inside? What makes you feel fulfilled? Answers to the above questions will help you discover the promise/dream/vision for your life. The things you say and do that bring you joy are an indication of the direction you should travel to reach your promise.

VI. HOW TO LIVE PROMISE DRIVEN LIFE

On one occasion Jesus said, "I am the True Vine." John 15:1 In other words, I am not just a vine or any vine, I am **The** Vine. The letter 'a' is an indefinite article referring to one of many of the same sort.   Whereas the word 'the' is a definite article referring to a particular one that is distinguished and set apart from others as the principle thing.

Jesus lived a promise driven life. And so, when He referred to Himself as '**The True** Vine', the metaphor is about a vine achieving its full potential and reaching its promise of all its branches bearing their most fruit, their best fruit at their highest level of fruit production. And once again, the picture of abundance and overflow emerges.

As this passage of scripture makes clear, the purpose of a branch is to bear fruit, and if it does not achieve its purpose, it is cut off.   But, the promise of a branch is to 'bear more and richer and more excellent fruit.' John 15:2(AV) However, as is always true about promise driven people, there is a price to pay to achieve the promise. The price for branches to achieve their promise is the painful process of "repeated cleansing and pruning." John 15:2(AV)

If we see ourselves as the branches – which Jesus intended – we should see the frequent prunings as metaphoric problems and challenges that are necessary to achieve our promise. In other words, each challenge we face and overcome represents a pruning that makes us more productive. Each problem you confront and successfully solve, is a pruning that makes your future fruit even richer. **In a promise driven life the painful process of pruning is viewed as part and parcel to achieving the promise.**

A promise driven person understands that every level of life has attitudes, beliefs and conduct that must be purged away in order to go to the next level. For example, you cannot play professional football with high school or college football attitudes, belief systems and conduct. The high school and college set of attitudes, behavior and conduct must be purged away in order to achieve and succeed in professional football. No matter how much satisfaction, comfort and/or pleasure gained from high school and college performance levels, they must be purged away to go to the next level. You cannot reach higher levels with lower level attitudes, beliefs and conduct. As already indicated, the purging process is painful, but necessary to achieving your promise.

In His choice of metaphor and conversation about His statement, "I am the true vine", Jesus makes it clear that **there are no shortcuts to promise** or the achievement of full potential. Inherent in His statement about being the 'True Vine' is a seven-step process that takes you from the problem of no fruit, to the purpose of fruit, to the promise of "much" fruit. This process, as indicated in the Introduction, is the pattern that promise driven people follow.

Step One: *Commitment*

The vine must be planted by the gardener. The promise/dream/vision to which you commit comes from God. Once God unveils and identifies your promise (dream/vision), you must commit to it. Promise driven people are steadfast. They are determined to reach their full potential. They are keenly aware of the extremely challenging nature of the path to promise. The path to promise has many casualties along the way. And the casualties are those who are not committed. They are those who are not completely convinced that the dream comes from God, that it is for them and that it's achievable.

The path to promise requires picking up your cross. **The path to promise cannot be traveled half-heartedly. If you are not fully engaged, fully involved and fully consumed by your promise (dream/vision), you will be side-tracked and detoured.**

Numbers 14:22-24 (NIV), ..."Not one of the men who saw my glory and the miraculous signs I performed in Egypt and in the desert but who disobeyed me and tested me ten times – not one of them will ever see the land I promised on oath to their forefathers ... But because my servant Caleb

95

has a different spirit and follows me wholeheartedly (fully), I will bring him into the land he went to..." Caleb and Joshua were promise driven people. They knew God's promise, declared God's promise and were committed to reaching God's promise for their lives.

To achieve what God promises, you must follow God fully. **A promise driven life follows God fully or wholeheartedly. A promise driven life requires passion.** It is characterized by fire, excitement and enthusiasm. In fact, with people of promise, people working towards all they can be, there is rarely a dull moment. There is always something going on. There is always something to do. There is usually always something happening. This is how commitment translates.

When committed to something, you steadily and consistently work on making it happen. The degree of difficulty of achieving your promise (dream/vision) demands the steadiness, steadfastness and consistency of commitment. When the ten other scouts were sowing seeds of fear, uncertainty and doubt with a negative report that contradicted God's promise, in Numbers 13:30, Caleb silenced the people before Moses and said, "We should go up and take possession of the land for we can certainly do it."

Commitment means determination. And people of promise are determined.

Commitment means resolve. And people of promise have resilience. No matter how tough things get or how big the challenges get or how long the problems last, promise driven people remain committed and are ready to take action consistent with their commitment. **Promise driven people have committed themselves to their dream and are determined to live it.**

This step involves asking yourself the following self-assessment type questions: How bad do I want to achieve my promise? Do I **really** want to live my dream? Do I really believe my dream is possible? Am I willing to go through what I must go through to achieve my promise? Am I able to accomplish this? Answers to these questions will give you an indication of how strong is your commitment and determination to live your dream. Short, decisive answers in the affirmative reflect the appropriate level of commitment for success. Caleb and Joshua gave a short, decisive answer in the affirmative to the concerns, complaints and questions about how powerful the opposition was, how fortified the cities were, and how weak and inadequate the Israelites were. They simply said, in Numbers 13:30, **"Let's go get it, we can do it."**

Promise driven people are direct. They don't talk a lot. They certainly don't talk to hear

97

themselves talk or to draw attention to themselves. They talk when necessary and say what needs to be said.

Promise driven people are decisive. Their decisions are based on alignment with their dream. If what is being considered is consistent with and advances their dream, the decision is easy and quick.

Promise driven people are positive. They tend to come down on the side of "yes I can" or "yes we can". They are optimistic and have a positive outlook on life.

How do you strengthen your commitment? **First, realize commitment is an intangible, spiritual quality.** It is akin to faith, resolve, resiliency, determination, desire and self-discipline. Commitment is a matter of belief. It is a matter of faith.

Faith tracks together with love. **When you truly love someone or something you are not afraid of committing to it. Your commitment to someone or something is increased as your love for that someone or something is increased.** 1 John 4:18 says, "There is no fear in love; but perfect love casts out fear..." Fear and doubt are opposites to and subtractors from faith and commitment. So, again, increase your love for someone or something and you will increase your commitment to it.

How do you increase your love? This takes us to the next point. **Invest in it.** Invest time, money, resources, effort, energy and sweat. The more you invest in someone or something, the more connected to it you become. And, the more connected you are to something, the more it becomes who you are and what you want to do and therefore, the more committed you are to it. Third, **decide to pursue** your promise/dream/vision. Remember, you may be only 50% successful in achieving what you do pursue. But, you will be 100% successful in not achieving what you do not pursue. Decide to pursue your promise and watch your commitment increase as you invest more of yourself and your resources.

David is one of the promise driven people in scripture. At one of the lowest moments of his life, he had to make a decision about whether he would continue to pursue his promise. At a time when most people would prefer to just sit and sulk at least for a while, David was told by God to pursue the enemy that had stolen everything from him and his men. In 1 Samuel 30, on returning to their temporary home in Ziklag, David and his men found that it had been raided, ransacked and burned to the ground. Additionally, all their wives, children and family members were gone. Their loved ones were taken. Their accumulated materials were missing, and their homes were burned to the ground. David and his men cried so hard and so long until they had no more strength to cry. They were so distraught and so distressed that bitterness set in. Then, when the bitterness set in, things got worse for David. His own men turned on him and began talking about stoning him.

Bitterness is quite distracting. It distracts you from your promise. It distracts you from your commitment to your promise. It distracts you from God. Problem driven people are prone to bitterness. Even purpose driven people can occasionally succumb to the burden of bitterness. Bitterness (anger and discontent) cannot only slow, it can stop your progress towards your promise. When things go wrong, as they sometimes will, don't allow bitterness to take hold. Remember and revisit your commitment. Use the occasion to grow, develop and get better. **Don't get bitter, get better.**

Every promise/dream/vision comes with a path attached. In this world you don't get something for nothing unless you are cheating. When God gives you a promise/dream/vision there's a path to it and the two cannot be separated. You cannot get the promise without the path. And, when you pursue the path you will reach the promise. I see the path as the "if" and the promise as the "then". The promise is God's part. Traveling the path is our part.

It is encouraging to note however that, if the promise comes from God and the attached path comes from God, the problems on the path belong to God. The problems on the path do not come from God, but since it's God's path, they belong to God and God is obligated to inspire a solution. What this means then, is **on the path to promise, God is with you. He is with you to assure your successful journey.** The issues, challenges, problems and enemies that occur along the path may be bigger than you but they are not bigger than God.

When problems pop up on the path to promise, first turn to God. That's what promise driven people do. They turn to God. When a tsunami of challenges turns your life upside down with overwhelming pain, agony and anguish, first turn to God. Don't start looking for someone or something to blame. Blaming, accusing and finger pointing solves nothing. It takes time and effort. It fosters unforgiveness and bitterness. It creates disunity and disconnection. And it adds to the time and effort required to get back onto your path to promise.

When David's men became bitter, they started focusing on and blaming him. Meanwhile, David who was in the same situation with his men turned to God. He did not revolve around and wallow in the problem. He did not get into a dysfunctional, disconnecting, back and forth argument with them to defend his position. David turned to God. He turned to the source of his promise. He turned to God and asked, shall I pursue this raiding party?

Will I overtake them? (1 Samuel 30:8 NIV) God's answer was, "Pursue them, you will certainly overtake them and succeed in the rescue." (1 Samuel 30:8 NIV)

God is a 'go forward' God. On the path to promise God is always about making progress. Even and especially when you are overwhelmed and inclined to sit and sulk. Since God's promise is so far out in front of you, so much bigger than where you are, so much better than where you are and so far beyond where you are, it stands to reason that the problems on the path will also be quite large. **In fact, I believe the depth of your pit is an indication of the height of your peak provided you remain committed to and continue the pursuit of your promise.**

It is very important to notice that God's answer and David's quest was to 'pursue them', that is the raiding party – the enemy – that had stolen their families, fortunes and future. God did not tell David to pursue his wives, children, materials and livestock. He told him to go after what had stolen his wives, children, materials, and livestock, defeat them, and his wives, children, materials and livestock would be recovered. This is an important distinction because it identifies why so many people never reach their promise. We want God's promise for our lives but we don't want to deal with the "raiding party/enemy" that has stolen it or distracted us from it.

Today the "raiding party/enemy" that has stolen our promise or distracted us from it is more likely to be internal. Things like laziness, indifference, complacency, fear, uncertainty, doubt, and worry are the most likely enemies that will rob us of our promise. These are the enemies that must be pursued. They must be pursued, overtaken and defeated. These enemies never completely go away. They are always lurking somewhere nearby. They are always ready to slip in and steal promise and/or distract us from it. Critical to achieving your promise is pursuing, overtaking and defeating these internal enemies. It is in this pursuit that we continue to build the necessary strength and wisdom to achieve our promise.

Pursuit is a reflection of commitment. The kind of pursuit that characterizes promise driven people would be better described as perseverance. Because of the ever present possibility of the internal enemies of laziness, ignorance, indifference, complacency, fear, uncertainty, doubt and worry, perseverance, the most intense level of pursuit, is required.

It's important to remember that the promises of God are just that – promises. This means, they already belong to you. They are already yours and the only way you can loose them is to allow them to be taken or stolen from you. The strength and wisdom to protect and hold onto them comes from the practice of pursuing, overtaking and defeating the enemies who will steal them. Promise driven people understand this and behave consistently.

When the 'spirit of God' moved in Genesis 1:2, God was committing to the creation of humans not heaven and earth. But the first step was to bring into existence the life-sustaining environment necessary to support humans. **God's commitment was to what He loved.** Then He proceeded to deal with everything preventing or impeding the achievement of that to which He was committed. What prevailed until God committed to creating humans was shapelessness, chaos, disorder, emptiness, purposelessness, fruitlessness, waste, darkness, no vision, no information, no knowledge, no light and no revelation. Because of God's commitment to creating humans, each of these impediments had to be successfully handled. This is what commitment means.

Commitment is a pledge or a promise to do something. God did not commit to creating humans provided the chaos and disorder were not too severe, or provided the darkness was not too great or provided He did not have to deal with a great deal of waste. God committed to creating humans despite having to deal with shapelessness, emptiness, darkness and the length of time it would take.

Commitment is a desire to accomplish what you set out to do that is greater than

the desire to avoid what you must go through. This means, to be sustained, love must be the object of commitment. **Love generates commitment. What you love you are committed to. When you love you are committed. Love is commitment. Commitment is love.** This point is made clearly and best in 1 Corinthians 13:4,7,8, "Love is patient. Love is kind. It always protects, always trusts, always hopes, always perseveres. Love never fails." (NIV)

To live a promise driven life requires commitment. Commitment requires love. You must love God's promise for your life more than your desire to avoid what you have to go through to achieve it. Your love for your promise/dream/ vision must be great enough for you to be willing to go through whatever is necessary to achieve it.

The only true test of commitment is results. If you want to know where your commitment is, examine your results. **Commitment gets results.** Commitment perseveres, protects, provides and never fails.

People are the point of creation. People are the object of God's love. God put himself into people. Genesis 1:27 says, "God said, let us make people in our image, after our likeness... and let them rule... over all the earth." God loved, was committed to, and poured himself into humankind. What we love we commit to. What we commit to we put ourselves into.

Along the way towards the achievement of His promise and commitment to create humankind, God took time to assess His results. Periodically, God assessed His progress/results and declared "it was good." Then, He continued. His progress/results along the way were 'good' all the way to His crown of creation – the human being. **A good product outcome requires a good process. If the process is good, the outcome will be good. The process is good when it makes progress towards the promise/dream/ vision.**

The activity of exercise is a good way to examine why commitment is necessary and how it is expressed in the life of a promise driven person. The first consideration is, what is the object of love? Promise driven life is healthy in spirit, mind and body. Though spirit is the strongest, each component feeds into the other. The love focus of a promise driven person is health, healing and wholeness. Exercise is not the focus. Exercise is a process by means of which we make progress towards what it is we love and want, health, healing and wholeness. Exercise is work. It requires the expenditure of serious effort and energy. It is a challenge that must be faced to achieve the health and well being we love.

A great question is, can you feel well and be well without exercising? And, the obvious answer is, yes. However, you will not be or feel your best. Promise driven people reach for their highest and best in all areas of life. They understand all areas of life are interrelated and indeed, interdependent.

Exercise builds physical strength, enhances cardiovascular effectiveness and efficiency, burns calories and helps manage weight, increases joint strength and flexibility, expands lung capacity, elevates mood and helps fight depression, helps manage blood sugar, contributes to slowing the pulse and lowering blood pressure, and increases self-esteem. All of these results contribute to the promise of overall health, healing and wholeness.

Health is necessary for the wholehearted pursuit of your promise/dream/vision. People want to be healthy. God's word promises health, healing and wholeness. 3John 2 says, "Beloved, I wish above all things that you may prosper and be in health, even as your soul prospers."(KJV) Matthew 15:30 says, "Great crowds came to him (Jesus), bringing the lame, the blind, the crippled, the mute and many others, and laid them at His feet; and He healed them."(NIV) Exodus 15:26 says, "If you listen carefully to God and do what is right in His eyes and pay attention to His commands and keep His decrees, I will not bring on you any of the diseases I brought on the Egyptians, for I am the Lord, who heals you."

To achieve the promise of health requires commitment. Commitment to health means you are willing to go through what's necessary to achieve it. And if exercise is one of those things, you exercise.

Promise driven people are clear about what their promise/dream/vision is. They practice, rehearse and repeat it as often as necessary to remain focused. **Focus strengthens commitment.**

Seven Days of Devotion to Commitment

Spiritual Principle to focus on is LOVE.

DAY 1: Loving God

Scripture: Mark 12:30

Word for the Day: LOVE

Other Scriptures: 1 Corinthians 13:4-8
Romans 12:9-10, Hebrews 13:1
1 Peter 1:22, 1 John 4:7
John 13:34-35, 1 John 2:7-11

Affirmations:
- "God is love."
- "I must love fellow human beings as I love myself."
- "God loves me just as I am."

Suggested Activities:
- Take time to be with God.
- Set aside time and place each day where you separate from business, noisiness, interruptions and distractions and just focus on the awesome love of God.

- Establish a sanctuary at home. Practice 'sanctuary' with God.
- Go out of your way to be kind to everyone you make contact with today.
- Practice kindness.

Notes to myself:

DAY 2: Hearing from God

Scripture: Psalm 46:10

Word for the Day: PEACE

Other Scriptures: Genesis 37:5, Colossians 3:15
Exodus 3:1-4, Philippians 4:7
Lamentations 3:25-26
Psalm 37:7, Daniel 6:10
Isaiah 26:3, 1 Kings 19:12
Hebrew 3:15

Affirmations:
- "I must be still to hear from God."
- "Peace, be still."
- "I am at peace."
- "I will be peaceful."
- "God is peace."

Suggested Activities:
- As you 'sanctuary' with God, ask God to make clear to you your gift and promise.
- Reflect on your life and explore what brings you joy.
- Ask family and friends for feedback on areas they think you excel in.

Notes to myself:

<u>DAY 3</u>: Living for God

Scripture: Romans 8:38

Word for the Day: DETERMINATION

Other Scriptures: 1 Corinthians 15:58
Philippians 3:12-14
Romans 14:8, Psalm 146:2
Psalm 63:4, John 6:67-69
2 Corinthians 6:3-10
2 Corinthians 5:7
Romans 4:18-24

Affirmations:
- "I will live for God."
- "I will live by faith."
- "I am determined to be healthy."
- "I am determined to make and stick with healthy choices."

Suggested Activities:
- Determine and practice making right choices for your spirit, mind and body.
- Start eating healthy.
- Manage your weight.
- Start an exercise routine and implement it at least 3 days a week for at least 30 minutes to an hour per session.
- Begin reading more. Read more scriptures.
- Memorize a scripture a week.

114

Notes to myself:

DAY 4: Enduring for God

Scripture: Romans 8:37

Word for the Day: RESILIENCE

Other Scriptures: Romans 8:28-31
Romans 8:35-36
Philippians 4:13

Affirmations:
- "I can do all things through Christ who strengthens me."
- "With God, I'm tough enough to handle the stuff that comes my way."

Suggested Activities:
- Do something or start something you have always wanted to but have never done.
- Start something you thought you could not do, but have always wanted to do. Begin with something small and simple like baking a cake or making a reconciliation call to a family member or an enemy.
- Do something you don't want to do but you know it would be a good thing to do.

Notes to myself:

DAY 5: Pursuing God

Scripture: 1 Samuel 30:8

Word for the Day: PASSION

Other Scriptures: Numbers 13:30, Exodus 14:15
James 4:7-8, 10, Jeremiah 20:9
Nehemiah 2:17-18
Revelation 2:4-5
Philippians 3:12-14
Hebrews 10:32-36

Affirmations:
- "I must go get my promise. It will not come to me."
- "My promise will not come to me. I must go get it."
- "Pursuing God is pursuing the godly."
- "Pursuit requires passion."
- "I am passionate about my pursuit of godliness."
- "I must be passionate about my promise."

Suggested Activities:
- Identify something you've talked about doing that you know you've been procrastinating on. Begin doing it.
- Clean and rearrange a section of the house or garage.

- Take a course or go back to school to learn more about what you do or a whole new area of activity.
- Put fire back into your marriage.

Notes to myself:

<u>DAY 6</u>: Focusing on God

Scripture: Joshua 1:8

Word for the Day: FOCUS

Other Scriptures: Psalm 1:1-3, Psalm 119:15-16,
Psalm 119:2, 105
Mark 12:30

Affirmations:
- "What I give attention to, I grow."
- "I grow what I give attention to."
- "I must give attention to God's promise for my life to grow its presence in my life."
- "My promise requires my focus."

Suggested Activity:
- Spend at least fifteen to twenty minutes on three separate occasions reading, meditating on and/or memorizing the above scriptures.

Notes to myself:

<u>DAY 7</u>: Achieving for God

Scripture: Matthew 25:21

Word for the Day: RESULTS

Other Scriptures: Galatians 6:7-10
1 Corinthians 15:58
Jeremiah 17:7-8, John 15:1-8

Affirmations:
- "I must get results."
- "The only true test of commitment is results."
- "My results reflect my commitment."

Suggested Activities:
- Only take on tasks for which you can commit to achieve results.
- Eliminate activity, projects and involvements for which you have achieved little to no results and where prospects for results are not good.

Notes to myself:

Step Two: _Accountability_

Jesus is known as the great "I Am". Jesus defines himself. Jesus declares who He is to all who will listen. His declaration is based on conversation between Him and God. In scripture God is the source of promises and dreams and visions designed to bless people. God gives promises (dreams and visions) to people based on their ability and willingness and willfulness to carry them out.

The second step in achieving promise is to declare specifically what it is. This is a statement of intention, a proclaiming of your aim. It should be stated in the affirmative, first person singular, present indicative of "I am". For example, in this instance Jesus says, "I am, The True Vine". He was expressing what was, by promise (dream/vision) of God, already a reality, though many were yet to appreciate it. The "I am" statements of Jesus like "I am the way, truth and life", "I am the light of the world", "I am the bread of heaven", "I am the good shepherd", "I am the door" and "I am the resurrection and the life" are all reflective of the words spoken by God to Moses in response to Moses' question, what shall I tell the people is your name? In Exodus 3:14 God says, "I am who I am. This is what you say to the Israelites: I am has sent me to you."(NIV)

In the eyes of God, with the help of God, we are whoever we need to be, and we can do whatever we need to do to achieve His promise. 'Am' is a statement of being and becoming. **Jesus was so connected to God and His promise (dream/vision) that He only referred to Himself in the context of God's promise.** Therefore He constantly used "I am" statements in reference to the promise of God for His life. And so, **Step Two in becoming a promise driven person is being clear about what is your promise (dream/vision).**

Ask yourself the questions: What specifically is my dream? What would I like to accomplish in life? What great achievement do I privately harbor and only occasionally share? What is the greatest contribution I can make with my life? What brings me the most joy when I think about doing it or accomplishing it? What great achievement do I daydream about frequently? What comes to mind when I think about what I would most like to do in life? What comes to mind when I think about what I can do best in life? Answers to these questions will help you unveil and identify God's promise (dream/vision) for your life.

Once identified, like Jesus, formulate your 'promise' into an affirmative, first person singular, present indicative statement. For example, if your dream is to "build a multimillion dollar, broom-making business" or to "be the best mechanical engineer in America" your statement would read, "I am the owner of a multimillion dollar, broom-making business" or "I am the best mechanical engineer in America."

The purpose of making and rehearsing this dream affirmation to yourself and repeating it to others is threefold. **First, it establishes accountability.** It says to the world what you want to be held to or judged on. The observation of others of your integrity to your promise (dream/vision) should help keep you on task and on target.

Second, the "I am" promise (dream/vision) affirmation shapes and reshapes your attitude or mindset. The conscious fruit of who you are and what you do is seeded and rooted in your subconscious mind. Attitude and mindset are the subconscious seed and roots that lead to the fruit of conscious thoughts, behavior and activity. The best mechanical engineer in America must have an attitude of the best. The owner of a multimillion dollar, broom-making business must have a multimillion dollar, broom-making mindset to make it happen. However, attitude and mindset are firmly established and rooted in our subconscious mind.

Attitude and mindset include things like our impressions, beliefs, self-images and values. All of these things result from and are stored in our subconscious mind along with all of our experiences and memories of life since early childhood. It is estimated that 85-95% of our mind is subconscious and the remaining 5-15% is conscious. The conscious mind – the smallest part – is where our thinking, awareness, reasoning, choosing, judging, and deciding goes on. The thinking, awareness, reasoning, choosing, judging and deciding that's going on in the conscious mind is based on and flows from the beliefs, impressions, images, values, attitudes and mindset that reside in our subconscious mind. Therefore, for your attitude and mindset to be shaped or reshaped, your affirmation must be repeated over and over and over again.

This step flows from affirmation, to attitude, to action, to accountability. Affirmations are consciously stated and repeated so as to impact our conscious and subconscious attitudes and mindsets. Then, our attitudes and mindsets determine our actions and activity directions. And, it is for our actions that we are held accountable.

Your accountability begins with your affirmation. You must repeatedly affirm your promise/dream/vision in order for it to positively impact your subconscious mind where your beliefs, values, impressions, attitudes and mindsets are rooted and housed. For an affirmation to become an attitude and eventually an action for which you are accountable, it must impact your subconscious mind.

According to Richard Kimball in his 9/21/08 website article, "The Power of Our Subconscious Mind", on his website: Building a Successful Life, it has been estimated that our conscious mind only holds about seven pieces of information in short-term memory, whereas the subconscious mind contains the storage of all acquired and accumulated knowledge, readings, thoughts, images, imaginations, messages, and memories. Researchers have further estimated that the unconscious mind outweighs the conscious mind on a scale of ten million to one. Further, Vince Poscente, in his book, "The Ant and The Elephant", published in October 2004, equates the conscious mind with the size of an ant on the back of the elephant-sized, subconscious mind. The image of an ant on the back of an elephant paints a vivid picture about the difference in size and potential impact on the human condition of the conscious and subconscious mind.

This helps us understand that changing your mind is not as simple or as easy as it sounds. To really change your mind you must impact your subconscious mind. To impact your subconscious mind you must use your conscious mind to actively change your thoughts. And, **repeated thoughts lead to actions. Repeated actions lead to**

habits. Repeated habits construct your character.

The process of going from affirmation to accountability is Step Two on the journey to a promise driven life. It involves affirming to yourself and others what you love and are committed to; reflecting this affirmation in your attitude and mindset; taking action consistent with your attitude and affirmation; and being accountable or willing to be judged by how consistent your actions are with your affirmation. The affirmation to accountability process is pictured in scripture.

John 1:1, 3 says, "In the beginning was the word (idea, concept, thought, accountability) and the word (idea, concept, thought, accountability) was with God and the word (idea, concept, thought, accountability) was God. All things were made by Him (idea, concept, thought, accountability) and without Him (idea, concept, thought, accountability) nothing was made that was made."(KJV) I believe this is saying, everything made or created begins with a thought. Repeated thoughts lead to the actions that build.

This passage of scripture could also read as follows: "In the beginning was accountability and accountability was with God and accountability was God. Through accountability all things were made; without accountability nothing was made that has been made. In accountability there was life, and that accountability was the light of men." Romans

12:2 says, "...be not conformed to this world but be transformed by the renewing of your mind..."(KJV)

In other words, to change your mind you must renew your mind. To renew your mind you must think new and different thoughts. And, you must think them repeatedly. Think them. Speak them. Write them down. Post them all around. Begin by affirming two things: 1) I am a promise driven person; 2) I am (...statement of your promise/dream/vision). Do this at least seven times (more is even better) a day for seven days a week over the next seven weeks (49 days). Watch, take note of, and appreciate the change that occurs and then continue.

The third reason for making and rehearsing this dream affirmation to yourself and repeating it to others is, it outlines actions. **Promise driven people take actions that are consistent with their promise no matter how distant, difficult or demanding is the promise.**

There is an expression I've used on an occasion that says, "Blessed are they that expect nothing for they shall never be disappointed." **People with low aims, don't experience high achievement.** High achievement is what God wants, expects and even promises for His people. We are all His people. High achievement is where abundant life is. Jesus came so that we could experience "abundant life."

If life in abundance is God's promise, why do so many settle for so little? Fear! Fear, uncertainty and doubt plague people and keep them from declaring and reaching for their promise. We express to ourselves fear generating questions like, "What if I fail?" "What if I fall on my face?" "What will people think or say about me if I don't make it?" "What if I lose everything?" "What if I can't take it?" "What if I don't make it?" "What if I make a mistake?" "What if it is not what I thought?" "What if I reach it and can't keep it?" These questions and others like them prevent people from aiming for and proclaiming the promise/dream/vision God has given them.

The fear, uncertainty and doubt reflected in these questions cause people to aim low and proclaim little in life. **When you aim low and proclaim little you're not accountable for much, and, you will not achieve much.** So, your risk of failure and/or embarrassment is low.

The step of accountability may be better understood through the following story. Imagine someone coming to you with three gift wrapped packages. Each package is beautifully wrapped and the same size. Each package also has a label describing its contents. Each package is being offered to you as a gift, but you can select only one. The three packages are labeled as follows:

#1 Ten Million Dollar
    guarantee and the path to achieve it.
#2 One Hundred Thousand Dollar
    guarantee and the path to achieve it.
#3 One Thousand Dollar
    guarantee and the path to achieve it.

The choice is yours. You can have any one of the packages, but you can only select one. Other rules apply to the packages as well. First, if you don't like or become uncomfortable with the demands of your package, you can downgrade it automatically, on your own without consulting with the gift giver. But, to upgrade to a higher level package you must consult with the gift giver.

It seems reasonable to me that every normal person confronted with this choice would select the package labeled "Ten Million Dollar Guarantee". Why? It's the richest package by far. With this package you can do more, go more, have more, help more, save more, and build more. With this package you can reach more, teach more, touch more, stretch more and bless more. Since all the packages have the same contents in different amounts, they can be measured and compared based on those contents.

Why would anyone decide to select less than the highest and best when it is readily and equally available from the gift giver? Why do people decide to live beneath their privilege? Why do people become comfortable and complacent? Why do people settle for the ordinary, the average and less than average? Why would someone, on purpose, aim low and proclaim little? I think the answer in a word is, accountability.

In the three package analogy above, the gift giver is God. The packages represent life choices and each of us is a recipient with the opportunity to choose.

Inherent in accountability is responsibility. Responsibility means work. It's been my experience that people want progress. People feel progress is a good thing. It is also known that progress requires change. For progress to occur, things must change. "Things" cannot change. People can. And, when people change they change things. To change requires effort. Change is serious work. This is one of, if not the main reason why, change is so difficult. Life is much simpler and easier without having to go through the effort necessary to make change. People don't like to change and people don't like change. People resist change. People even resist change that will make things better for everybody. This is especially so when the proposed change threatens existence, benefits, recognition, power or authority.

Progress requires change. Everybody wants progress, but nobody wants to change. This is why change is so hard to come by and progress takes so long.

Accountability Steps Up

Accountability steps up, into and breaks this cycle. Accountability steps up and steps into issues that threaten to compromise and/or curtail achievement of promise. Accountability assumes responsibility and takes charge. Promise driven people are accountable. They step up and into issues that threaten achievement of promise. They assume responsibility and take authority.

When David came to visit his brothers who were on the front lines of the war with the Philistines, he was not a soldier, he was not in the army and he was not there to join. However, when he got there and experienced Goliath's threats towards God, he assumed responsibility, took charge and took on Goliath. When the twelve leaders returned from scouting the promised land, they began to give a very negative report. Caleb and Joshua interrupted, assumed responsibility, took charge and gave their positive but minority report.

A prominent characteristic of promise driven people is, they step up. They don't have to be begged or pleaded with. They don't have to be argued with or convinced to do something. When it comes to living their promise/dream/vision they are ready and willing to do what's necessary to help make it happen. They are like Isaiah who said, "Here am I, send me." They don't hesitate to step into the realm of accountability. They are quick to recognize not only that something needs to be done, but also, that they are first in line to do it.

Promise driven people struggle like anybody else. In fact, promise driven people often struggle more than others with bigger challenges than others. However, the difference between the struggling of promise driven people and problem driven people is one of substance. The struggles and challenges of promise driven people are about things that alter environments and shift paradigms. Whereas the challenges and struggles of problem driven people are over things that don't change their focus on problems.

When a struggle of a promise driven person is over they are promoted or elevated in status, position, fruitfulness, increase, wealth, strength, power or authority. When the struggle of a problem driven person is done, they are usually in the same spot or worse. **The path of promise driven people courses them in the direction of life changing challenges. In other words, the path of promise driven life is so challenging it changes the person.**

The path of problem driven life is feeling and immediate gratification oriented. Once the problem is addressed or the feeling is better, they remain unchanged and continue on their way until the next problem occurs.

The irony of accountability is, you are accountable for whichever life direction you choose. **Promise driven people understand the level of their life direction does not change their level of accountability.** It seems reasonable to me that since I am totally accountable anyway, it may as well be for something of great value. Don't continue to struggle over nothing. This makes no sense. For, after a hard struggle or fight, you will have nothing to show for it.

Be accountable for something worthwhile. So that even if you're not as successful in your struggle as you'd like, at least you'll have the peace of mind that comes from knowing you fought for something of great value and gave it your best shot. Decide today to step up to some major disorderliness in your life, or some major emptiness in your life, or some major darkness in your life and affirm the change that you will make.

Promise driven people are characterized by accountability. They are willing to be accountable. They step up to challenges. They assume responsibility, take authority, and are always active. Their actions are consistent, pointing in a certain direction. That direction is toward their promise.

Accountability Has Direction
Promise driven life has direction. Sometimes the direction is not all that plain and

clear to see and understand even to the person, but promise always has direction. A dream always has a direction. **Accountability has direction.** The direction of accountability is toward promise/dream/vision. This is why it is so important to have a dream for your life. A dream for your life must be clear and specific. Otherwise you don't really have a dream. Your dream/promise must be clear and specific. Otherwise how do you know what to work on or what direction to go in.

Clarity and specificity characterize true promise. God is clear and specific. One of the ways you determine that your promise/dream/vision comes from God is how clear and specific it is. God wants His people to be clear about His promise. God wants His people to be clear about the direction He desires. God wants His people to achieve His promise, not theirs. So, as I mentioned in the introduction, when God gives a promise/dream/vision, it is always clear and specific. This is so that the direction to its achievement will be plain and simple. Plain and simple does not mean smooth and easy.

It is worth repeating here what the prophet Habbakuk says about a promise/dream/vision that comes from God: "Write down the revelation and make it plain on tablets so that a herald may run with it. For the revelation awaits an appointed time; it speaks to the end and will not prove false. Though it lingers, wait for it; it will certainly come.

(Habbakuk 2:2-3 NIV) This passage of scripture speaks to the importance of clarity, specificity, and certainty. When it comes to your promise/dream/vision, God is clear, specific and certain. When God gives a promise all three of these points come into play.

Accountability demands clarity and specificity. Without clarity and specificity what is there to be held accountable for? The point of clarity and specificity is accountability. Without them there is no way to measure progress or monitor direction. In fact, without clarity and specificity there is no direction and can be no progress. **Promise driven life has clear and specific direction.**

God gave Noah the promise/dream/vision of starting a whole new world. God outlined for Noah a clear and specific path to the achievement of this promise. God gave Noah His promise/dream/ vision of building an ark. Noah was not a ship builder. He had no experience with boats, let alone one the size God was talking to him about. So God had to be clear and specific to be sure of Noah's direction and results. In Genesis 6:14-16 God gives Noah a set of specific instructions: "Make yourself an ark of cypress wood; make rooms in it and coat it with pitch inside and out. This is how you are to build it: The ark is to be 450 feet long, 75 feet wide and 45 feet high. Make a roof for it and finish (make a window) the ark to within 18 inches of the top. Put a door in the side of the ark and make lower, middle and upper decks."(NIV)

Without clarity and specificity from God regarding His promise, humans are inclined to insert what would feel better to them, and be more convenient and easy. It would have been easier for Noah to build a small rowboat. It would have been even easier to not build a boat at all. But Noah lived a promise driven life. He determined that the direction of his life would be toward the promise/dream/vision that God gave him. And that promise – to start a new world – was worth whatever he had to go through to make it happen.

Noah was clear as we should be today, **there are no shortcuts to glory. All shortcuts to glory are cut short.** God presented Noah with a promise/dream/vision of being the vehicle for starting a new world. Noah stepped up. He assumed responsibility, took authority, got started and was accountable.

God gave Moses the promise/dream/vision of living a God centered life. God outlined for Moses a clear and specific path to the achievement of this promise. The path attached to the promise involved the building of a tabernacle and began with bringing the appropriate offerings. God was clear and specific about the types of offerings, what to use them for, how to use them, and where to place them so that the tabernacle would be built exactly according to God's instructions. After giving

Moses a specific listing of the types of offerings required (Exodus 25:1-7), God then says to Moses in verses 8-9, "Make a sanctuary for me and I will dwell among you. Make this tabernacle and all its furnishings exactly like the pattern I will show you." Then in chapters 26, 27, 28, 29, 30, 35, 36, 37, 38, 39 and 40 extensive specific detail was provided so that there was no room for questions or guessing about how to build God's tabernacle and live a God centered or promise driven life.

Moses stepped up. He assumed responsibility, took authority, got started and was accountable. Promise driven people make things happen. Moses was a promise driven person. Exodus 39:42-43 says, "The Israelites had done all the work just as the Lord had commanded Moses." Moses inspected the work and saw that they had done it just as the Lord had commanded.(NIV)

So many people are so unclear about God's promise for their life, it is easy to understand why so few people are living promise driven lives. In fact, I think it's safe to say that a substantial majority of people are so bogged down and consumed by the immediacy of day-to-day problems they have no clear and specific promise/dream/vision from God. I am convinced of this because so many people are unable to articulate their promise/dream/vision with any clarity or specificity. Some are worse off than having no clearly articulated promise/dream/vision, they have no idea at all. It is no wonder that so many people

141

wander aimlessly through life in pingball fashion being bounced from one problem to another. **If your life is not being driven by promise it is being driven by something else that is less than your promise.**

Turn to God, hear from God, listen to God and say what God says about you. Speak over your life. Speak over your life what God says. Affirm what God says, not what your circumstances and problems say. Repeatedly affirm to yourself the greatness that God has placed in your spirit and speaks to your soul. Step up to your highest level of accountability. Ask God to make your promise/ dream/vision clear. Then, don't question it, just go for it. If God gives it to you, you can do it.

Seven Days of Devotion to Accountability

Spiritual Principle to focus on is FAITH.

DAY 1: My promise:
- distinguishes me.
- makes me stand out.
- is clear and specific.

Scripture: John 15:1

Word for the Day: DISTINGUISHED

Other Scriptures: Genesis 12:1-3,
Galatians 1:15-17
Genesis 6:8-9, 14-16
Isaiah 49:1, Jeremiah 1:5
John 6:35, 10:9, 10:11, 11:25
14:6, 15:1

Affirmations:
- "I was born to make a difference."
- "I am here to make a positive difference."
- "I will make the difference I was born to make."

Suggested Activities:
- Ask family and friends what distinguishes you; what makes you stand out.
- Spend time reflecting on what you think distinguishes you or makes you stand out.

Notes to myself:

<u>DAY 2</u>: My promise is challenging.

Scripture: 1 Corinthians 15:57

Word for the Day: VICTORY · VICTORIOUS

Other Scriptures: Romans 8:37, Philippians 4:13
Ephesians 3:20

Affirmations:
- "My faith will give me the victory."
- "By faith I am victorious."
- "I am a winner."
- "I have the power."
- "I am an overcomer."

Suggested Activities:
- Meditate on and memorize the above scriptures.
- Find and reach out to people who have overcome great odds to achieve greatness in their lives and seek out their secrets or methods of success or overcoming.

Notes to myself:

<u>DAY 3</u>: My promise must be declared/ spoken/affirmed to myself and others.

Scripture: Acts 4:13, 19-20, Habbakuk 2:2-3

Word for the Day: BOLD · BOLDNESS

Other Scriptures: John 6:35, 10:9, 10:11, 11:25, 14:6, 15:1

Affirmations:
- "I will declare and attempt great things for God and expect great things from God."
- "I will make the difference I was born to make."
- "I will do and be my highest and best."
- "I will live my promise."

Suggested Activities:
- Frame and outline your promise to your personal satisfaction.
- Then, tell somebody about your promise and deal with their reaction.
- Write your promise out and post it around your home and office.

Notes to myself:

<u>DAY 4</u>: I must believe my promise is for me and that I can achieve it.

Scripture: Matthew 25:14-15

Word for the Day: FAITH

Other Scriptures: Hebrew 11:1
2 Corinthians 5:7
James 2:17, 26

Affirmations:
- "If God gave it to me, I can do it."
- "If I can conceive it and believe it, I can achieve it."

Suggested Activities:
- Take some action towards your promise.
- Make at least a small step.
- Start reading and learning about what it is.
- Talk with others who have done it or something similar.
- Ask God to increase your faith.

Notes to myself:

<u>DAY 5</u>: My promise requires taking the initiative and acting.

Scripture: James 2:17, 26

Word for the Day: WORK · RESPONSIBILITY

Other Scriptures: Galatians 6:7-10
1 Corinthians 15:58

Affirmations:
- "I was made to work."
- "I am responsible."
- "Faith works."
- "My promise will be achieved by working at my highest and best."

Suggested Activities:
- Take a walk in a park or in your neighborhood and notice the things of nature: Sun, Atmosphere, Trees, Bushes, Ants, Bugs, Flies, Birds, Dogs, Cats, Bees, Squirrels, Worms, Fleas, Clouds, Grass, Flowers, Water.
- Notice that everything in nature works at its highest and best.
- Know that the work of nature gives us life.
- Be inspired to work at your highest and best.

Notes to myself:

<u>DAY 6</u>: My promise requires energetic obedience to God's Word.

Scripture: Proverbs 3:5-6

Word for the Day: OBEDIENCE

Other Scriptures: Psalm 37:23, 1 Samuel 2:9
Psalm 119:105, Psalm 1:1-3
Deuteronomy 6:3, 7:11-14, 28:1
Acts 5:29

Affirmations:
- "I am who God says I am."
- "I can do what God's Word says I can do."
- "I will do what God's Word tells me to do."
- "I give God praise by obeying His Word."

Suggested Activity:
- Identify one of the most challenging sermon lessons of your pastor, priest, imam or rabbi and begin implementing it in your life.
- Remember, your promise will challenge you to do something you think you cannot do.

Notes to myself:

<u>DAY 7</u>: My promise requires humility.

Scripture: Matthew 16:24, Mark 10:45

Word for the Day: HUMBLE · SERVICE

Other Scriptures: Numbers 12:3, Matthew 5:5
Psalm 37:11, 147:6
Isaiah 29:19

Affirmations:
- "I will be selfless."
- "I am a good steward."
- "I am here to serve."
- "I must be humble."
- "Promise driven people are humble."

Suggested Activity:
- Volunteer to help the less fortunate through your church and/or other nonprofit organizations.
- This should be a regular and consistent activity.

Notes to myself:

Step Three: _Preparation_

The vine must be nourished. **Promise driven people prepare.** And they constantly improve. **No one can achieve their full potential without preparation and constant improvement.** This step involves study, information accumulation and training. Study nourishes. Study improves. Study prepares. In scripture it is quite clear that all of God's promise driven people were prepared. They were nourished and strengthened by the preparation that comes from serious and intense study, prayer and work. They prayed a lot. They were in constant communion with God.

God prepares people by giving them a promise they must prepare for, giving them a mind to prepare and allowing them to be in situations that provide valuable experience necessary to achieve promise. For example, Joseph was given a dream/promise. He was also sold into slavery, falsely accused of rape and incarcerated. These very challenging situations afforded him the time and opportunity to study and completely depend on God.

Moses spent the first forty years of his life learning the system that oppressed his people. Then, he spent the next forty years hiding on the backside of the desert shepherding sheep and learning lessons that would help him lead his people. Moses spent eighty years in preparation for the final forty years he spent reaching for God's promise.

Paul, on the road to doing what he was doing, was blinded, given a new and different charge (promise/vision), then went off and separated himself to prepare. Galatians 1:15-18(a), "But when God who set me apart from birth, and called me by His grace, was pleased to reveal His Son in me so that I might preach Him among the Gentiles, I did not consult any man, nor did I go up to Jerusalem to see those who were Apostles before I was, but I went immediately into Arabia and later returned to Damascus. Then after three years, I went up to Jerusalem"...(NIV)

Noah, a farmer, and one of God's promise driven people, had to be in constant communion with God to successfully complete the building of the Ark. Noah had achieved his purpose as a righteous man of God. Building an Ark was not only something new for him, it was far beyond anything he had ever done before. The idea to build the Ark came from God. Because of the state of the world, the bad state of the economy, the large number of wars, the wide prevalence of evil and self-indulgence, Noah could see (through God) where things were headed (Genesis 6:17, ...everything on earth will perish). So, God gave Noah a vision (Genesis 6:14, "So make yourself an Ark"). The vision was a promise

(Genesis 6:18, "I will establish my covenant with you and you and your family will enter the Ark"). And Noah's life was driven by that promise from that point on (Genesis 6:22, "Noah did everything just as God commanded him").

To achieve his promise, Noah had to be nourished by God. He had to be guided by God. He had to follow God. To follow God he had to be in communion with God. This meant frequent prayer.

While prayer is communion with God, work is the highest form of prayer. **The highest level of communing with God is working for God.** God prepares you to work for Him.

God is spirit. So God represents our highest and best effort to achieve our highest and best. Spending time with God is nourishing. Spending time with God is studying and listening to His Word. Spending time with God is preparation for achieving His promise. Spending time with God is spending time reflecting on your highest and best effort to achieve your highest and best. God's promise for you is your most, highest and best.

Noah was prepared by God to achieve his highest and best because "Noah walked with God", Genesis 6:9(NIV). This means Noah believed in God, behaved in God, spent time with God, studied God, listened to God and lived for God.

In Step Three, examples of initial questions to be asked include the following: What training do I need to raise my skill level? What skills do I need to achieve my promise (dream/vision)? What do I need to improve? Do I need to go to school or go back to school? Do I need to get a degree? What do I need to know?

Studying, preparing, planning and thinking about your promise is part of what it means to live a promise driven life.

The vine must grow and develop. Development is a stage in growth or advancement. To develop is to cause to become gradually fuller, larger and better. Development occurs by pushing forward, by moving, by taking action.

Promise driven people find a way to move forward toward the promise no matter what is facing them. For promise driven people the promise takes precedence over all problems. When the people of Israel arrived at the Red Sea they saw the awesome army of Pharoah approaching them from the rear and "they were terrified, cried out to God, and said to Moses, 'You brought us to the desert to die?' What have you done to us by bringing us out of Egypt?" Exodus 14:10-11 (NIV) Moses told the people to be still and stand firm in God. He told them to stand in and on the promise of God.

When you stand on the promise of God you are standing on your highest level, in

your best position, in your strongest and most powerful place. Then God said to Moses, "Why are you crying out to me? Tell the people to go forward." Exodus 14:15 (NIV) **God is a "go forward" God.** Development is going forward. Going forward is development. God is a god of growth and development.

Promise driven people know that you cannot achieve your promise – which is much larger than you – by remaining at your same small size. You must grow and develop in the direction of your promise. Growth and development best occur when you go forward. When caught between a sea of uncertainty about your future and sought by the sword of certain slavery from your past, God says, go forward.

The greater the uncertainty you succeed in managing, the greater the growth that results from movement. Promise driven people know, nothing substitutes for taking action. No amount of thinking, studying, planning and preparing, as important as all of these are, can substitute for taking action. **Faith not acted on is not faith. To know and not do is to not know. You cannot think your way into a new way of behaving, you must behave your way into a new way of thinking.** In other words you must be born again.

You must experience a new birth. You must become a new creature with a **d**ivine **n**ew **a**genda (DNA). New creature DNA results from your new birth. New birth occurs when you begin taking new and different action at new and different levels.

Procrastination is an enemy of progress and therefore, an enemy of promise. Procrastinators do not achieve their promise. Promise driven people understand that procrastination kills progress and promise. To procrastinate is to put off doing something until later; to defer taking action. In short it means to put off doing. To postpone. When you put off doing, you put off movement. When you put off movement, you put off progress. When you put off progress, you put off your promise. Caleb could sense the people were getting ready to put off going forward. So, when their tone was getting increasingly negative, Caleb spoke up and said in Numbers 13:30, "Let us go up **at once** and possess it (the promised land)." (AV) Similarly, when David faced Goliath, his greatest challenge yet, he did not procrastinate or hesitate. 1 Samuel 17:48 says, "As the Philistine (Goliath) moved closer to attack him (David), David **ran quickly** toward the battle line to meet him (Goliath). (NIV) David and Caleb lived promise driven lives.

Additional questions to ask yourself in Step Three include: Am I making progress? Am I moving forward? Am I closer to my promise this day, week, month, year, than I was yesterday or last week, month or year? What movement can I make? What step can I take? How can I move forward?

Every day should be seen and appreciated as an opportunity to prepare, grow or develop toward the achievement of your God-given promise/dream/ vision. You nourish your promise/dream/vision by paying attention to it. **What you pay attention to, you grow.** This works on both the positive and the negative side. Just like you can grow the presence and position of the promise for your life by paying attention to it, you can also grow the presence and position of problems. Things that can be done daily to give attention to and nourish your promise/dream/vision include: reading, clipping and saving relevant articles, conversing with an expert in the field, writing a paragraph, a page or two about the achievement of your promise. Begin or complete reading a book about it.

When your promise/dream/vision is beyond your ability to prepare for it, it is fantasy, a daydream, an illusion, and comes from you, not God. **The promise/dream/vision that God gives is always a big stretch, but it is always achievable.** It always involves major preparation, growth and development, but it's always achievable. It requires serious energy, work and effort but it's achievable. **Promise is always far bigger, better and beyond where you**

are. And so, by definition, it requires the energy, work and effort of serious preparation to be reached. **Preparation is necessary to reach your promise, and to keep it.**

The preparation necessary to achieve your promise stands on your commitment to it. People prepare for what they are committed to. Jesus said in Matthew 16:24, "If any will come after me let him deny himself, pick up his cross and follow me." Since all of the promises of God are fulfilled in Jesus, this could be read another way. It could be read, "Whoever wants to pursue their promise must prepare him/herself, practice self-discipline and be committed."

Preparation is future oriented. It always looks to the future. You never prepare for something that has already taken place. You prepare for what's coming up, what's going to happen, what is scheduled to occur, what you want to take place. And, your level of preparation is inextricably intertwined with your level of success.

This point is emphasized by coaches to athletes. Teams can play only at the level for which they have prepared. Entry level preparation will result in entry level play. Championship level preparation will result in championship level play. You cannot prepare at entry level and expect to play at

165

championship level. In terms of academics, honor roll, honor society, merit scholar preparation is very different from passing grade preparation. And similar to athletics and the rest of life, you cannot prepare at the passing grade level and expect to achieve honor society results. **Promise driven people prepare at the level of promise.**

Preparation is, getting ready. It is making ready, equipping, furnishing or fitting out. Better yet, preparation is the **process** of making ready, equipping, furnishing or fitting out. Studying is the process of making ready for an exam. Practicing is the process of equipping yourself with the skill to play an instrument. Reading is the process of furnishing your mind with an expanded awareness.

Promise driven people prepare. They understand preparation is an ongoing process, as promise often unfolds over time as you move forward. The more you prepare, the closer you walk with God, and the farther you walk with God, the more of Himself God reveals to you.

Preparation (which includes learning, growth, development and practice) is an extremely challenging – for many, the most challenging – step in achieving promise. Everybody loves the glory that follows high achievement. But few fully appreciate the preparation necessary to get that glory. Most people prefer to look for a short cut to glory, settle for looking at (on television, computers, movies) others bask in their glory, or look for ways and opportunities to stand in the light of another's glory. I believe God is grieved by so many of His creation deciding to not push for their promise. God is grieved by so many of His creation settling for standing or sitting around discussing others' glory. I further believe that preparation is one of, if not the most, major reason for this decision. Preparation is hard. It requires serious self-discipline. There is no getting around it. You cannot ignore it. No one else can do it for you. It requires **your** time, **your** energy, **your** effort, **your** work and **your** focus. You can neither avoid it, nor can you delegate it. If **you** do not do it, it is not done. As I said earlier, preparation is one of, if not the main reason, why so many of God's creation decide not to pursue their promise.

Each of us is born with a great amount of innate potential. The full achievement of this potential (promise/dream/vision) brings with it the appropriate and commensurate glory. Jesus said in His prayer to God in John 17:4, "I have brought you glory on earth by completing the work you gave me to do."(NIV) The "work God gave Jesus to do" was placed in Him as innate potential. It was Jesus' decision to live it out or not. Jesus lived out His full potential (promise/dream/vision) and experienced the appropriate and commensurate glory.

The innate potential of humans is "the work that God gives us to do." The only way to maximize our God given human potential is through the required energy, effort, work and focus of preparation. And, again, this involves reading, repeating, researching, studying, thinking, problem solving, and practicing. These things can be difficult. They require serious self-discipline, and they take time. **The key to getting people** (including and especially young people) **to prepare, or want to prepare is, finding their promise. Peoples' behavior changes when they love what they want to do more than they dislike what they have to go through.**

Ask yourself, "Am I preparing for anything?" "What am I preparing for?" "Am I enthusiastic about my preparation?" These questions help you to identify what your promise is and/or whether or not you are living a promise driven life.

You prepare for promise by learning and practicing being "faithful over a few things." The parable of the talents makes clear that the route to being "ruler over many and big things" is being "faithful over a few things." Promise driven people make a habit of making the most of whatever they've been given. Promise driven people don't have pity parties when the hand they've been dealt is a poor one. They make the best of it. They view a poor hand as preparation. It is preparation for a big and powerful hand. They understand that how you handle little, lack, limitation and scarcity is an opportunity to practice how to achieve and handle much, abundance and prosperity.

Promise driven people learn to view and approach obstacles, hard tasks, hard times, trials and trouble as preparation. They understand the path to promise is preparation for promise and preparation for promise is the path to promise.

Seven Days of Devotion to Preparation

Spiritual Principle to focus on is PATIENCE.

<u>DAY 1</u>: My promise requires prayer.

Scripture: 1 Thessalonians 5:17

Word for the Day: STRENGTH

Other Scriptures: Philippians 4:6, Nehemiah 4:9
Matthew 6:25-34

Affirmations:
- "I am getting stronger every day."
- "I am gaining strength each day."
- "Prayer brings power."
- "Prayer prepares me for my promise."

Suggested Activities:
- Pray frequently.
- Pray frequently for your promise.
- Pray at least three times a day – morning, noon, night.
- Practice praying spontaneously – on the spot.

- Practice having conversations with God like you are conversing with a friend or neighbor.

Notes to myself:

<u>DAY 2</u>: My promise requires planning.

Scripture: Nehemiah 2:11-16

Word for the Day: PLAN

Other Scriptures: Luke 14:25-33
Jeremiah 29:11

Affirmations:
- "I plan to succeed."
- "I am planning to be victorious."
- "I plan to win."
- "I am planning to be a champion."

Suggested Activities:
- Set aside time to think about your promise/ dream/vision.
- Work on developing a road map including goals, objectives, strategies and activities.
- Write the plan down.
- Revisit and revise the plan every six months, if necessary.
- Remember, the plan is dynamic and flexible not static and rigid.

Notes to myself:

<u>DAY 3</u>: My promise requires practice.

Scripture: Psalm 1:1-3

Word for the Day: PRACTICE

Other Scriptures: Joshua 1:8; Proverb 3:5-6
Psalm 119:16; 35; 105

Affirmations:
- "Practice makes perfect."
- "Practice pulls me towards my promise."
- "Repetition is the essence of learning."

Suggested Activities:
- Reflect on this thought: Anything done at the level of promise (highest and best) must first be practiced at the level of promise.
- Do your very best at whatever you do today. For example:
    - Be your best, loving, smiling, warm self to all you interact with.
    - Greet people with a warm smile all day, no matter what.
    - Offer to do extra at work.
    - Go out of your way to be kind to all people you interact with – family, friends, coworkers and strangers.
    - Give the right-of-way to other drivers.
- Repeat this on day 4,5,6,7.

Notes to myself:

<u>DAY 4</u>: I must grow into my promise.

Scripture: Matthew 4:19

Word for the Day: GROWTH

Other Scriptures: Genesis 12:1-3

Affirmations:
- "Every day in every way I'm getting better and better."
- "I am growing."
- "I am better today than yesterday."
- "I will keep getting better."

Suggested Activities:
- Identify an area of weakness in your prayer life, planning or practice and take steps to strengthen it or make it better.
- Identify a positive habit of someone more successful than you at what you want to do, and begin to practice and grow that habit.
- Identify what needs to change in you to facilitate growth into your promise, e.g. mindset, attitude, self-worth, thinking. Take steps to address these.

Notes to myself:

DAY 5: I must be equipped for my promise.

Scripture: Nehemiah 2:4-9

Word for the Day: PROVISION

Other Scriptures: Philippians 4:19; Psalm 23:1
John 10:11

Affirmations:
- "When God gives a vision He makes provision."
- "God gives vision and provision."
- "I am provided for."
- "God is my Shepherd, I lack nothing."
- "God is my source. He will provide."

Suggested Activities:
- Identify a skill necessary to achieving your promise and take a course to learn it.
- Seek training that will raise your level of proficiency.
- Become technologically literate.
- Pursue technological sophistication.

Notes to myself:

<u>DAY 6</u>: I must make continuous progress towards my promise.

Scripture: Exodus 3:10

Word for the Day: PROGRESS

Other Scriptures: Exodus 14:15; Judges 6:14
Matthew 28:18-20

Affirmations:
- "God is a 'go forward' god."
- "I must make progress."
- "I will continuously improve."
- "Everyday I will get better and better."

Suggested Activity:
- Measure the distance you traveled; the difference you've made toward your promise since yesterday.

Notes to myself:

<u>DAY 7</u>: My promise speaks to my future.

Scripture: Jeremiah 29:10-11

Word for the Day: HOPE

Other Scriptures: Genesis 12:1-3; Matthew 4:19

Affirmations:
- "I am always hopeful."
- "In God my future is secure."
- "My hope is built on God."
- "I will never give up on my promise."
- "I must never give up."

Suggested Activities:
- Reflect on your level of optimism.
- Are you optimistic about life in general and your promise specifically?
- Ask family, friends, coworkers, associates and neighbors if they see you as optimistic.
- Collect, consider, weigh and digest the information for an honest assessment of your level of optimism, and thereby, how much hope you have.

Notes to myself:

Step Four: _Maturity_

The vine must produce branches. Branches on a vine suggest growth and development to the point of maturity. Branches indicate both a readiness and capacity to produce and reproduce. The promise driven person is a mature person with both the readiness and capacity to produce and reproduce. How do you know when you are mature? You know you are a mature, promise driven person when:

1) **You neither procrastinate nor hesitate** to tackle challenges much larger than you. For example, David did not procrastinate or even hesitate to take on Goliath. Noah did not procrastinate or hesitate to build the Ark. Abednego, Shadrach and Meshach did not procrastinate or hesitate in speaking the truth of their God to the power Nebuchadnezzar of Babylon. In Daniel 3:16-18, the three Hebrew youth confronted with bowing down to worship a man or being thrown into a fiery furnace to their death, said, "O Nebuchadnezzar, it's not necessary for us to answer you on this point. Our God whom we serve is able to deliver us from the burning fiery furnace, He will deliver

185

us out of your hand, O King. But if not, let it be known to you, O King that we will not serve your gods, or worship the golden image which you have set up."

2) **You remain faithful through adversity.** Despite many and frequent opportunities to doubt God and His promise (dream/vision) Joseph remained faithful. And it was quite clear that "God was with Joseph". (Genesis 39:2) Most of us can be faithful when the sun is shining and things are going well. But it takes maturity to be faithful through adversity. God's promise driven people are faithful through adversity. **Promise driven people, because of their faithfulness, prosper even while dealing with adversity.** Promise driven people do not have pity parties because of big problems. **Promise driven people approach problems like they are strength-building exercises necessary to mature them in the direction of achieving their highest and best.**

Joseph lived a promise driven life. Genesis 39:1-3 says, "Joseph was brought down to Egypt; and Potiphar, an officer of Pharoah, the captain and chief executioner of the royal guard, bought him from the Ishmaelites who brought him down to Egypt. But the Lord was with Joseph and he (though a slave) was a successful and prosperous man; ...and his master (Potiphar) saw that the Lord was with him and that the Lord made all that he did to flourish and succeed in his hand."(AV) Though sold into slavery by his siblings, Joseph's behavior and service remained consistent with his promise. Joseph (a promise driven person) understood that because of the distance, difficulty and demands of achieving the promise (dream/vision) of God, any deviation would be a major setback and could possibly take him off track all together. So, even when things got worse and Joseph was thrown into prison, his behavior remained consistent with achieving his dream (promise/ vision). He continued to work at his highest and best. He continued to work like he was at the top of the class though his circumstances had him at the bottom of the barrel. He continued to work like he was in charge, in control and responsible for the well-being and welfare of the lives of the people around him. Genesis 39:20-23, "Joseph's master (because of the lying words of his wife) put him in prison. But the Lord was with Joseph and showed him mercy and loving kindness and gave him favor in the sight of the warden of the prison. And the warden committed to Joseph's care all the prisoners and all there was to do in the prison. The warden paid no attention to anything that was in Joseph's charge, for the Lord was with him and made whatever he did to prosper."(AV)

Promise driven people shape their circumstances to be consistent with their promise. They alter their environment along the lines of their dream. The point here is the circumstances and the environment don't do the shaping and altering, the people do. The people are driven by the passion generated by the promise that comes from God.

3) **You exhibit boldness and daring.** Mature promise driven people will not back down from paradigm-changing challenges. For example, while all the disciples were achieving the purpose to which God called them – to follow Jesus by getting in the boat – Peter reflected boldness and daring by coming out of the boat and experiencing the paradigm-

changing, walking on water. Joshua, a noted and experienced warrior, used to fighting, showed boldness and daring in his belief in God by his obedience in not fighting but just walking around the walls of Jericho.

The promise (dream/vision) that God gives you is usually so far out in front of you that when achieved, it both changes the way you do things and it changes the things you do. Therefore, promise driven people, by definition, must have boldness. They must be daring. **To achieve promise you will have to go up against the prevailing winds of spiritual, psychological, social, political, educational and economical resistance.** These winds are very strong and represent conventional wisdom, the status quo, "the way things are done", the climate, the environment, or the system. Boldness and daring are required to go against these winds. You can recognize your level of maturity as a promise driven person by the levels and frequency of your experiences with boldness and daring.

The questions to ask to gain clarity with where you stand in your maturity as a promise driven person include: Am I a risk taker? Do I always play it safe? Have I ever stepped out on faith?

How do I evaluate and increase my maturity as a promise driven person? Practice stretching out and stepping out of your normal and routine pathways. For example: take a different route to work or just turn down a street you are unfamiliar with and see where it leads; call up a company for an appointment to tell them you have the product that meets their need like no other can; tell your dream to someone familiar with you; identify what differentiates you; explain to and convince yourself why you are a superstar; visit a stranger in the hospital and make him/her feel better; dress up (suit and tie; dress and heels) and go to a place where no one will see you (movie theater, your living room, local hardware store); dress down (jeans, sneakers and sport shirt) and go to a place where a lot of people will see you (church, office building); get in your car and go get lost.

How you feel during and how you handle the unfamiliar, the strange, the different, the disconcerting and the distressing are indicators of your maturity as a promise driven person.

The maturity of a promise driven person is reflected not only in ability to care for themselves, but further, in concern for others. **Promise driven life is not only fruitful, it helps**

others bear fruit. Greater maturity is indicated by greater numbers of people being helped to bear greater amounts of fruit.

Indeed, promise driven people who are mature, target helping others maximize their fruit. The ultimate purpose of the vine is to provide the branches with what they need to bear much fruit. **The spectrum of maturity ranges from the immaturity of being totally self-centered to the seasoned point of being sacrificially 'other' centered.** Where you are on this spectrum helps you identify how mature you are as a promise driven person. Additional questions to help you determine your level of maturity as a promise driven person include: Am I a good listener? (I believe listening is the highest of the communication skills. I'm still pursing its mastery). Do things have to go or be my way in order for me to participate? How willing am I to give my time, talent and treasury to help others succeed? How do I feel when I am helping someone else get themselves together for success? Do I enthusiastically look for ways and means to help others or must I be reminded to even think about it?

Promise driven people are always looking for opportunities to serve. They constantly ask the question, how can I serve? Or how can I help? This, of course, reflects Jesus whose entire focus was service. And not just service, but totally 'other' centered, sacrificial service. Jesus said, "Whoever wants to become great among you must be your servant and whoever wants to be first must be your slave – just as the son of man did not come to be served but to serve and to give his life as a ransom for many." (Matthew 20:26-28 NIV)

Promise driven life serves. It protects, provides for, and prospers others. The promise God gave to Noah of starting a whole new world was primarily focused on saving others (his family). The promise God gave to Joseph, though initially it seemed to be all about his elevation, turned out to be for the protection, provision and prospering of not only his family but also the Egyptians. The promise God gave to Moses on the backside of the desert, was entirely focused on and for the benefit of the people of Israel. The promise God gave to Paul was for the benefit of "the Gentiles." Jesus said about Paul, "This man is my chosen instrument to carry my name before the Gentiles and their kings and before the people of Israel. I will show him how much he must suffer for my name." (Acts 9:15-16 NIV)

In each of these instances, Noah, Joseph, Moses and Paul, serving others was a primary focus of their promise. Even more than just serving others, each of these men was called on for sacrificial service to others. They experienced severe hardship on their path to promise.

This gets to the heart of why maturity is essential to living promise driven life. Achieving promise is always extremely challenging. It's never easy. Without maturity you would not be able to serve and continue to serve as necessary. Promise driven life must be mature. Testimony to this point is Paul's life experiences after receiving, accepting and committing to God's promise. Paul described his situation by saying, "We put no stumbling block in anyone's path... rather as servants of God we commend ourselves in every way; in great endurance; in great troubles, hardships and diseases; in beatings, imprisonments and riots; in hard work, sleepless nights and hunger; in purity, understanding, patience and kindness; in the Holy Spirit and in sincere love; in truthful speech and in the power of God; with weapons of righteousness in the right hand and in the left; through glory and dishonor, bad report and good report; genuine yet regarded as impostors; known, yet regarded as unknown; dying and yet we live on; beaten, and yet not killed; sorrowful, yet always rejoicing, poor yet making many rich; having nothing, and yet possessing everything." (2Corinthians 6:3-10 NIV)

Maturity is required to go through all this and stay on the path to promise.

Maturity recognizes the promise/dream/vision that God gives, and knows its importance. It recognizes the value of promise and knows there's no higher calling.

Maturity is the wisdom to know that those most in need of help may give you the most trouble.

Maturity is strength to keep pushing towards promise through personal difficulty because you understand its part and parcel of the path to promise.

Maturity resists any and all feelings of bitterness towards those being served even though they may be the source of personal difficulty.

Maturity always turns to God for help.

Maturity is preparation, growth and development to the point of readiness and capacity. Readiness (willingness) and capacity (ability) are important. You cannot have one without the other and be mature. Both are needed.

How is maturity developed? Where does it come from? How do you get it?

First, pursue it. Pursue capacity building preparation, growth and development. Make a decision to be involved in continuous learning. Read, take free courses, study, talk with experts, spend time doing mind expanding activities (museums, documentaries, historical site visitations). All of this will help you reach your promise.

Next, practice serving. Volunteer. Look for ways and means to involve your volunteer time and service, especially in an area consistent with your promise. For example, if you believe your promise is in the field of medicine, there are large numbers of volunteer opportunities from which extremely valuable experience and expertise can be gained. There are hospitals, clinics, doctors' offices and medical research facilities.

Finally, be a keen observer of people. Pay attention to the way people behave. Study human behavior. It is especially important to notice and study the behavior of those who have been successful in the area of your promise. What did they do? How did they do it? Which direction did they take? How long did it take? How much did it cost? How are they handling it? Knowledge and expertise, with how to work with, lead, manage and organize people are invaluable and make a giant-sized contribution to maturity.

Maturity is best achieved through working with people. Nothing seasons one's experience and expertise like working with people from all kinds of perspectives and backgrounds. Promise driven people are willing to work with all who are willing to work. They will even work with people unwilling to work in an effort to make them willing to work. Much of the maturity of promise driven life is both achieved and reflected in a willingness to work with all who are willing to work. Maturity is gained by taking on and succeeding at the challenge of dealing with difficult personalities and producing positive results.

Seven Days of Devotion to Maturity

Spiritual Principle to focus on is
RIGHTEOUSNESS · PEACE

DAY 1: Mature, promise driven people have the ability to achieve promise.

Scripture: 1 Samuel 16:7

Word for the Day: YES, I CAN

Other Scriptures: Matthew 25:14-15

Affirmations:
- "I am able."
- "I can do this."
- "I can do what God has gifted me to do."

Suggested Activities:
- Seek opportunities to practice your gift.
- Get outside, neutral, independent, honest feedback on your activity.
- Learn and know what you can do (ability) and how much (capacity).

Notes to myself:

<u>DAY 2</u>: Mature, promise driven people are willing to fully engage life for the purpose of achieving their promise.

Scripture: Psalm 27:4

Word for the Day: DESIRE

Other Scriptures: Matthew 9:9
                              Matthew 4:19-20

Affirmations:
- "I want to live a life of promise."
- "I want to be a promise driven person."
- "I want to make the difference I was born to make."
- "I am ready to live my promise."

Suggested Activities:
- A positive attitude about life is always right.
- Identify areas where your attitude is negative and one by one rid yourself of the negative mindset.

  How? 1. Ask family and friends to help.
             2. Have them call to your attention any negative comments on the subject and challenge you with a positive one.

Notes to myself:

<u>DAY 3</u>: Mature, promise driven people are daring and bold.

Scripture: Acts 4:13

Word for the Day: BOLDNESS

Other Scriptures: 1 Samuel 17:32
Matthew 14:27-29

Affirmations:
- "I can do all things through Christ who strengthens me."
- "If I can conceive it and believe it, I can achieve it."

Suggested Activities:
- Set a bold goal for yourself for the day, week, month, quarter, 6 months, year.
- Go for it.

Notes to myself:

<u>DAY 4</u>: Mature, promise driven people are "other" centered.

Scripture: Philippians 2:3-4

Word for the Day: SELFLESS

Other Scriptures: Romans 12:10; Mark 10:45
Romans 12:3

Affirmations:
- "I am blessed to be a blessing."
- "I am here to help others."
- "Making things better for others makes things better for me."

Suggested Activities:
- Participate in conversation on subjects you're passionate about and just listen. Let others do all the talking.
- In a bank, supermarket or elsewhere, find out if someone in your line is in a hurry and give up your space to them.
- Identify ways you can promote or prosper someone else and seek opportunities to carry them out.

Notes to myself:

DAY 5: Mature, promise driven people are givers.

Scripture: John 3:16; 2 Corinthians 8:1-9

Word for the Day: GENEROUS

Other Scriptures: Mark 10:45; Luke 6:38

Affirmations:
- "Giving is living."
- "The more I give, the more I live."

Suggested Activities:
- Sacrifice and give more to your favorite charity.
- Give more time.
- Give more of your expertise.
- Give more money.

Notes to myself:

DAY 6: Mature, promise driven people endure.

Scripture: 2 Corinthians 6:3-10

Word for the Day: PERSEVERANCE

Other Scriptures: Psalm 30:5; 1 Corinthians 13:7
2 Corinthians 4:8-12
Hebrew 12:2-11

Affirmations:
- "Storms come to pass."
- "This too shall pass."
- "God is with me and will never leave me."
- "God will never leave nor forsake me."

Suggested Activity:
- Meditate on and/or memorize the following scriptures: 2 Corinthians 6:3-10; Psalm 30:5; 2 Corinthians 4:7-12; 1 Corinthians 15:58; 1 Corinthians 10:13; Luke 1:37; Matthew 19:26.

Notes to myself:

DAY 7: **Mature, promise driven people cooperate. They believe in teamwork, and know they're part of a team effort. They are principled but humble and easy to work with.**

Scripture: Romans 12:5; 1 Corinthians 12:12
Ephesians 4:16

Word for the Day: COOPERATION·
HUMILITY

Other Scriptures: 1 Corinthians 12:12-30
1 Corinthians 3:9
Matthew 18:4
James 4:6; Matthew 5:5
Numbers 12:3; Psalm 147:6
Psalm 25:9

Affirmations:
- "I am a member of the team."
- "Life is a team sport."
- "Excellence is my standard, cooperation is my method, humility is my anchor."
- "I am easy to work with."
- "I believe in and practice cooperation."

Suggested Activities:

- Set aside a time period (day, week, month) during which you will be totally, enthusiastically, and humbly cooperative in an organization or ministry you are very much involved in and feel strongly about.
  - Listen to and understand the suggestions and recommendations of others.
  - Willingly accept and enthusiastically perform your assignment.
  - Energetically do exactly what you are told exactly how you are told to do it.
- You can practice this in your marriage and/or family as well.

Notes to myself:

Step Five: Productivity

The vine must have its branches bear fruit. The purpose of the vine and its branches is to bear fruit. **Every promise (dream/vision) given by God is related in some way to productivity or fruitfulness.**

In Genesis 9:7-9 God says to Noah, "...be fruitful and increase in number; multiply on the earth and increase upon it. Then God said to Noah and his sons, I now establish my covenant with you and your descendants." In Genesis 17:1-2 when Abram was ninety-nine years old, God appeared to him and said, "I am God almighty, walk before me and be blameless. I will confirm my covenant between me and you and will greatly increase your numbers." In Exodus 19:5 God speaks to Moses and tells him to tell the people, "if you obey me fully and keep my covenant, then out of all nations you will be my treasured possession. Although the whole earth is mine, you will be for me a kingdom of priests and a holy nation." God said to David in 2nd Samuel 7:12-14, "When your days are done ... I will raise up your offspring to succeed you, who will come from your own body, and I will establish his kingdom. He is the one who will build a house for my name, and I will establish the throne of his kingdom. I will be his father and he will be my son."(NIV) Hebrews 9:15 adds the new covenant of Christ to this discussion as it says, "Christ is the mediator of a new covenant that those who are called may receive the promised eternal inheritance."

Further, 2nd Corinthians 1:20 says about Jesus, "For no matter how many promises God has made, they are 'Yes' in Christ. And so through Him the Amen is spoken by us to the glory of God."(NIV) **God's covenant promises, no matter who they are with, focus on increase, fruitfulness, productivity or being prospered.** God's covenant promises call for adding, multiplying and/or building the one with whom the covenant has been entered. God's covenant promises all speak to the productivity of people of promise. God adds, multiplies and builds them to the point where they can be and are a blessing to the lives they touch.

God is a god of covenant or promise agreements. A covenant is a binding agreement made by two or more individuals. It usually has an "if", "then" structure to it. For example, 2nd Chronicles 7:14, "**If** my people who are called by my name will humble themselves and pray and seek my face and turn from their wicked ways, **then** will I hear from heaven and will forgive their sin and will heal their land." The covenant, which is a mutual promise agreement, outlines the work assignment for both parties. The "if" portion is man's obligation and the "then" portion is God's. The "if" portion belongs to humans, comes first, and is always an uncertainty. The "then" portion belongs to God, comes second and is always a certainty. The structure of the "if", "then", covenant promise agreement helps to simplify, clarify and specify the way to live your promise.

People of promise are productive. In fact they are very productive. They are productive because:

1. **Productivity is a way of life** for them. It is the way they live and breathe and have their being. Promise driven people take seriously their portion of the "if","then" covenant promise agreement. They live by faith in the "then" portion. And their faith is reflected in their strict adherence to their "if". In fact, promise driven people convert their "if" portion to a life principle and live by it. For example, the "if" in 2nd Chronicles 7:14, "If my people who are called by my name will humble themselves and pray and seek my face and turn from their wicked ways..." becomes, "I am one of God's people so I will be humble, pray, seek God's face and turn from my wicked ways." And this principle becomes a way of life, which results in much forgiveness and healing.

2. **They are never daunted by difficulty.** They never let bad times

lower their level of effort or excellence. They don't let hard times, hard tasks, hard trials and hard trouble dampen or depress their attitude. They remain optimistic with a positive and upbeat frame of mind. **Promise driven people make the best of bad situations.** Joseph is a perfect example. He lived his life according to and consistent with his dream (promise/vision). That's what promise driven people do. They live life according to, and consistent with their dream even when their life experience is going through a nightmare. Though Joseph was a slave he was still the best steward he could be. He cared for his master's belongings like they belonged to him. Though Joseph was a prisoner he did his prison work at his highest and best. Though his circumstances changed drastically toward the worst, he never lost sight of God's promise and continued to work towards it at his highest and best. Even as a slave and prisoner, Joseph made a decision to stand out. He decided he would be the best at whatever he did. Joseph was a promise driven person. **Promise driven people don't fit in, they**

stand out. They are more productive than others, especially when times, tasks, trials and trouble are hard.

3. **They see productivity as the path to promise.** Being productive is the way to increase, multiplication, fruitfulness, a bigger and better life. People of promise understand the scriptural prescription, "if you are faithful over a few things, I will make you ruler over many things." Matthew 25:21(NIV) People of promise turn this into a simple principle statement, "I will be faithful over a few things." When this principle guides your life you rarely, if ever, have a pity party. And you're always found doing good though things for you may be going bad. Promise driven people are productive because they remain faithful when they have 'a few' or 'little'. Hard times, tasks, trials and trouble are typically characterized by having "a few" or "little". And you are challenged to do the same and more with 'less', 'a few' and 'little'. **People of promise are faithful stewards of their 'less', 'little' and 'a few'. Thus they never miss an opportunity to increase or be increased, to**

add or be added to, to multiply or be multiplied.

The questions to be asked in this Step include: Am I energetic and enthusiastic about my dream? Do I still get fired up when discussing my dream? Do I have pity parties in hard times? If so, how often? How long? Do I really believe my dream came from God? Do I believe God? What kind of attitude do I have? Do I use my attitude and behavior to shape my circumstances or do my circumstances shape my attitude and behavior? What have I accomplished? Do I get things done? Am I a finisher? Can I work with people? Do I get things done through people?

After creating humans, the first thing God says to them is, "Be fruitful and multiply/increase." Being productive is a central theme of scripture. From Genesis to Revelation, God charges His creation to be productive. God Himself is the first model of productivity. The very first words of the Bible speak to God's productivity as Genesis 1:1 says, "In the beginning God created the heavens and the earth." (NIV) And this theme continues all the way to the last chapter of the last book in the Bible (Revelation) where it speaks about "the river of the water of life, as clear as crystal, flowing from the throne of God and of the lamb down the middle of the great street of the city. On each side of the river stood the tree of life bearing twelve crops of fruit, yielding its fruit every month. And the leaves of the

217

tree are for the healing of the nations." (Revelations 22:1-2 NIV)

Many scriptures, beyond the above bookend references, speak to the importance of fruitfulness. In Genesis alone, in addition to his own unlimited and continuous fruitfulness in producing the universe, "the world and they that dwell therein", God says of and says to Noah, Abram, Isaac, Jacob, Esau, son of Hagar and Joseph, "Be fruitful and increase." Essentially all of the major characters mentioned in Genesis were fruitful and increased in numbers, productivity, power, prosperity and wealth. In Genesis, from the very beginning God establishes His pattern and path to productivity.

Satisfaction with being unfruitful and unproductive is ungodly. Anyone satisfied with being unproductive, getting nothing done, doing nothing, achieving nothing, going nowhere, staying in the same place, experiencing no movement, making no progress, getting no promotion, is someone who not only will not, but, cannot reach their promise. These persons have yielded to and are being driven by a spirit of fear, uncertainty, doubt, laziness, ignorance or a combination of many or all of the above.

Promise driven people are fruitful. They are productive. They are this way all the time. They seem to know and understand:

They always have something to work with.

They can always make something happen.

Being productive is the rent we pay for our time and space on earth.

Being productive means improving the planet.

Being productive means making things better for other people.

They are distinguished by the kind and amount of fruit produced.

Productivity is how you leave a footprint in the sands of time.

Being productive is much more fulfilling than being unproductive.

Productivity is more fun than unproductivity.

How can productivity be increased? How can you increase your productivity? **First, be organized.** The first rule of heaven is order. To produce the heavens and the earth, God first had to establish order. Order is more productive than disorder or chaos. In fact, **chaos and disorder produce nothing but more of the same.** For productivity to take place at all, let alone at the level of promise, structure and function must be appropriately positioned. Light is more functional and productive than darkness. Shape or structure is more functional and productive than shapelessness. Meaning and purpose are more functional and productive than emptiness, voidness and no purpose or meaning.

Order is static. Organization is dynamic. Order is stationary. Organization moves. Order is rigid. Organization is flexible. Order is limitation. Organization is liberation. Order looks good. Organization is good. Order's focus is input. Organization's focus is output. Order can be death. For example, a corpse is quite orderly. Everything is exactly in place. Organization is life. And life can assume many different sizes, shapes and configurations, but all designed to produce.

Organization is the systemization of order. It is the institutionalization of the interconnection of appropriate structure and function. Order is the necessary first step towards its connection and formation as organization. Order is the necessary prelude to the life and productivity of organization. In other words, organization gives life to order. Organization causes order to be productive.

The more organized you are, the more productive you'll be. Be organized.

Next, be service-oriented or other-centered. You can increase your productivity by serving others. Serving others builds, grows, develops, supports and strengthens them to where they can be more productive. And when they produce more, so do you. When you serve others you are growing, developing, maturing and strengthening yourself. That's productivity. And additionally, as you serve others, they are being enabled to be more productive.

Promise driven people are characterized by organization and service orientation.

Third, learn to delegate. Delegation is one of the best ways to increase your production. Delegation is not as simple as it sounds. On the surface it would appear to be a simple and common sensible thing to do to increase one's productivity. **Delegation is simply getting others to help you get things done.** To the degree you are effective with this is the degree to which you will be more productive.

However, delegation can be difficult. Often there are many issues that must be dealt with. There is the tendency to want to do things yourself; the belief that your way is the only way and you are the only one who can do it like it is supposed to be done; the lack of trust in others you work with; the patience and perseverance in mentoring others to the level of maturity necessary to assume tasks that will contribute to overall productivity; and the failure to hold people accountable for their assignment.

Promise driven people understand that delegation increases productivity.

Promise driven people are characterized and recognized by a service attitude, organization and a willingness to delegate. Each of these things substantially increases productivity.

Seven Days of Devotion to Productivity

Spiritual Principle to focus on is JOY.

DAY 1: Promise driven people are faithful. Being faithful makes you fruitful or productive.

Scripture: Matthew 25:21

Word for the Day: FAITH

Other Scriptures: James 2:17, 26
2 Corinthians 5:7; Hebrew 11:1

Affirmations:
- "I am faithful over a few things."
- "I work."
- "I produce."
- "I will keep going and going and going."

Suggested Activities:
- Look back over today or this past week and list what you produced. Also, list the things you started but did not finish and got no results. You may also look back over a longer time period (month, year) and go through the same process.

- Identify why and how you were successful at producing what you did.
- Take note and rehearse these answers.
- Identify what you started but did not finish and why. Take note, so this can be corrected.

Notes to myself:

<u>DAY 2</u>: Promise driven people have an optimistic attitude.

Scripture: Philippians 4:19

Word for the Day: OPTIMISM

Other Scriptures: Psalm 23:1

Affirmations:
- "Yes I can."
- "I am productive."
- "I get results."

Suggested Activities:
- Take a day or two at first, then a week, and practice catching yourself in any and all negative comments about anything or anyone.
- Each time you catch yourself, stop, and turn the comment around to a positive one.
- Remember, no matter how negative a situation may be, there is always something positive about it. Look for it and state it!

Notes to myself:

<u>DAY 3</u>: Promise driven people are creative. They bring things into existence.

Scripture: Genesis 1:1; John 1:1-3

Word for the Day: CREATIVITY

Other Scriptures: Nehemiah 6:15; John 1:1-4, 14

Affirmations:
- "I am here to make good things happen."
- "I am here to make a positive difference."
- "I am here to make things better."
- "I make things better."
- "I am here to bring good things into existence."

Suggested Activities:
- Set aside 15 to 30 minutes each day for creative thinking.
    - You can do this alone or with others.
    - Think about your promise/ dream/vision.
    - List everything and anything that comes to mind about doing what you do differently, or, doing something different to accomplish the same thing.

228

- Prioritize the ideas/thoughts/ suggestions/concepts that surface.
- Select one, and explore its viability for implementation.
- Implement the creative idea.

• Practice using your less dominant hand for signing your name, picking up, carrying, placing and dragging things.

Notes to myself:

DAY 4: Promise driven people organize and prioritize their lives.

Scripture: 1 Corinthians 14:40
1 Corinthians 14:33

Word for the Day: ORGANIZATION

Other Scriptures: 1 Corinthians 14:40
Genesis 1:1-5

Affirmations:
- "I must be organized."
- "My promise is my priority."

Suggested Activities:
- Begin each day by developing a prioritized To Do List.
  - Start with #1 and get as far as you can.
  - The list could be categorized as follows:

	URGENT	NOT URGENT
IMPORTANT	Priority #1	Priority #2
NOT IMPORTANT	Priority #3	Priority #4

#1 Priority: Important and Urgent
#2 Priority: Important but Not Urgent
#3 Priority: Not Important but Urgent
#4 Priority: Not Important and Not Urgent

231

There may be several items in any given category that may have to be further refined but this should get you started.
- This same process could be followed at the beginning of each week, month, quarter, half-year, year.

Notes to myself:

<u>DAY 5</u>: Promise driven people are passionate about accomplishing or building something that makes a positive difference in the lives of others.

Scripture: Nehemiah 2:17

Word for the Day: BUILD

Other Scriptures: Genesis 1:31
Nehemiah 6:15
1 Corinthians 14:12
Ephesians 4:29

Affirmations:
- "I build"
- "I get positive results."
- "I make good things happen."
- "I am a builder."

Suggested Activities:
- Identify some things that you started but remain unfinished (e.g. painting a room, taking a course, reconciling a relationship, cleaning the garage or basement, implementing an exercise program, following through on a New Year's resolution, sending thank you notes).

- Prioritize them.
- Start with #1 and finish it.
- Identify something else and finish it.
- Be sure to include items that are big enough to require the help of others.

Notes to myself:

<u>DAY 6</u>: Promise driven people are passionate about accomplishing or building something that makes a positive difference in the lives of others.

Scripture: Nehemiah 2:17

Word for the Day: BUILD

Other Scriptures: Genesis 1:31
Nehemiah 6:15
1 Corinthians 14:12
Ephesians 4:29

Affirmations:
- "I build"
- "I get positive results."
- "I make good things happen."
- "I am a builder."

Suggested Activities:
- Identify some things that you started but remain unfinished (e.g. painting a room, taking a course, reconciling a relationship, cleaning the garage or basement, implementing an exercise program, following through on a New Year's resolution, sending thank you notes).
- Prioritize them.

- Start with #1 and finish it.
- Identify something else and finish it.
- Be sure to include items that are big enough to require the help of others.

Notes to myself:

<u>DAY 7</u>: Promise driven people are passionate about accomplishing or building something that makes a positive difference in the lives of others.

Scripture: Nehemiah 2:17

Word for the Day: BUILD

Other Scriptures: Genesis 1:31
Nehemiah 6:15
1 Corinthians 14:12
Ephesians 4:29

Affirmations:
- "I build"
- "I get positive results."
- "I make good things happen."
- "I am a builder."

Suggested Activities:
- Identify some things that you started but remain unfinished (e.g. painting a room, taking a course, reconciling a relationship, cleaning the garage or basement, implementing an exercise program, following through on a New Year's resolution, sending thank you notes).
- Prioritize them.

- Start with #1 and finish it.
- Identify something else and finish it.
- Be sure to include items that are big enough to require the help of others.

Notes to myself:

Step Six: _Expansion_

The vine must have dead branches cut off/away in order to bear more fruit and better fruit. Because the refinement process can be extremely difficult and painful, people rarely do it willingly, voluntarily and on their own. Humans usually must be **incentivized** somehow to cut out and cut away dead and unproductive attitudes, beliefs, behaviors, habits and desires.

Refinement occurs over the course of a hard time, task, trial or trouble. **Hardship is part and parcel of the path to promise.** Hardship is essential to the refinement process. It is during hardship that we are forced out of necessity to cut out and cut away anything that impedes us on the path to promise. During hardship we're forced to travel as light as possible. Loads that are too heavy cause us to slow, struggle, and even stop. However, the things we are carrying and holding on to mean something to us. This is why it's hard to willingly, get rid of them though they may be adding to or extending the hardship.

It's one thing to cut out a vacation trip or shopping for clothes, it's more challenging to cut away from certain people. It's hard enough to purge difficult people and circumstances at work, it's much harder when they are in your family. It's hard to cut out a bad work habit, it's much harder to cut out an addiction. Rarely do individuals seek the place of pain associated with the refinement process. Usually we just find ourselves there as a result of the direction we've been traveling.

Promise driven people know that refinement is necessary to achieve more fruit and better fruit. **Promise driven people view hard times, tasks, trials and trouble as refinement.** When you have done nothing to earn suffering, refinement is taking place. You are being made better, stronger, wiser, and smarter.

Consider the prophet Elijah, who, after announcing the drought and famine to King Ahab, was told by God to go east and hide by the brook Cherith. God said, "Drink from the brook and I have ordered ravens to feed you there." Then when the brook dried up, God told Elijah to "go at once to Zarephath and stay there. I have commanded a widow there to supply you with food."(1 Kings 17)

In both instances, the words God spoke to Elijah had to seem more than a bit far-fetched or outlandish. After all, how could birds feed you? Or how could a poor, destitute and hopeless widow feed him? Yet, in both instances Elijah did exactly what God told him. And exactly what God said would happen, happened. Elijah drank from the brook and ravens brought him meat in the morning and in the evening. Then at Zarephath, Elijah was provided for by a widow for the rest of the famine.

244

The word Cherith is derived from a Hebrew word that means 'to cut' or 'covenant'. The word Zarephath is derived from a Hebrew word that means "refinement" or, "to purge away". To connect or covenant with God requires 'cutting' the ties to anything that would prevent this from happening.

Probably the main thing that prevents a covenant connection with God is doubt. Doubt separates you from God. Doubt creates a distance between you and God (your highest and best self). Doubt denies the power of God. Doubt defuses your intensity. Doubt drains your energy. Doubt destroys your enthusiasm. Therefore, doubt deprives you of the opportunity to achieve your promise. Since the promise of God is the Word of God, the Word of God must be believed to achieve the promise of God. And, you cannot achieve what you do not believe.

Elijah believed the Word of God. Elijah trusted God. Elijah knew God. Elijah spent time communing with God. Elijah was in covenant with God. A covenant is a binding agreement between two or more individuals. Elijah was in a covenant partnership agreement with God such that, what God said, Elijah did. **What God says always includes what God will do if you do what He says.**

When Elijah agreed to go to the brook Cherith, he was agreeing to cut his ties to any doubt, and move forward in covenant with God believing that He would fulfill His promise to have 'ravens' feed him with meat in the morning and evening of every day. This could be looked at as the pruning process. Then, when things got worse and the brook dried up, God refined Elijah's faith. During a dire drought and famine God said to Elijah, 'Go at once to Zarephath' where he would be provided for by a poor, destitute, down to her last meal, convinced she and her son were going to die, widow. To trust God in this situation is the ultimate in the refinement of your faith. The processes of cutting out/away (purging) and cutting back (pruning) are both painful and representative of the refinement of your faith, which is essential to achieving the promise of God. All of God's promise driven people experience some variation of the painful refinement processes of purging and pruning on the path to promise.

Noah had to endure ridicule during sunshine as he built an Ark for unprecedented rain.

Abraham had to leave everything familiar and friendly to him to travel by faith through the dark to what was unfamiliar and unfriendly.

Joseph endured being sold by siblings into slavery, carried off to a foreign land, falsely accused of molestation and imprisonment for something he did not do.

Moses had to spend forty years on the backside of the desert tending sheep.

David had to spend years running for his life, living in a cave, as an outlaw.

Daniel was taken captive from his homeland, enslaved as a servant, subjected to a death sentence and thrown into a lions' den.

Hananiah, Mishael and Azariah were taken from their homeland as slaves, subjected to a death sentence, and thrown into a furnace of fire.

Refinement is the most painful step towards achieving your promise. It can last a short while or it can last quite a while. However, with the challenge associated with cutting out, cutting away and cutting back, even a short while becomes a long while. Refinement is necessary to achieving your promise. Said another way, **purging and pruning are prelude to promise.**

You cannot run your fastest, or jump your highest or do your best and most while carrying luggage of doubt, uncertainty, fear, worry, ignorance, low self-worth and esteem. Refinement (process of purging and pruning) gets rid of the luggage. It is through the refinement process that the luggage is cut out, cut away, and cut back. The refinement process usually involves a hard time, hard task, hard trial or hard trouble.

God is our gardener. He knows and determines the purging and pruning necessary to achieve promise. Suffering (hard times, tasks, trials, trouble) that is handled according to God's word/promise always leads to promotion.

Problems handled according to God's promise always lead to a promotion toward that promise.

The refinement (purging, pruning) process is for the purpose of learning how to solve problems according to the promise. **A promise driven person solves problems according to the promise. The promise is the end and the means. In other words, you have to act like you are there even though you are not there so that you can get there. Your behavior must be consistent with where you are headed or you will never get there.** Looked at from the vantage point of professional athletics, the best teams practice like they intend to play. The best teams realize you cannot play what you have not practiced. Nor can you play at a level you have not practiced. And so, problems can be viewed as the purging and pruning of practice that leads to play at the level of promise.

The three Hebrew youth, Hananiah, Meshael and Azariah were promise driven people. Their behavior led them to the adversity of the fiery furnace, but was so consistent with God's promise that people could see God with them. And as a result Daniel 3:30 says, "then the King promoted Shadrach, Meshach and Abednego in the province of Babylon."

Joseph was a promise driven person. He was sold to slavery in a foreign land, falsely accused of molestation, and imprisoned for years for something he did not do. Nevertheless he was so excellent in everything he did that both his slave master and prison warden could see that God was with him. Genesis 39:2-4, "The Lord was with Joseph and he prospered and he lived in the house of his Egyptian master. When his master saw that the Lord was with him and that the Lord gave him success in everything he did, Joseph found favor in his eyes and became his attendant. Potiphar put him in charge of his household and entrusted to his care everything he owned."

And in Genesis 40:20-23, "...while Joseph was in prison, the Lord was with him; he showed him kindness and granted him favor in the eyes of the prison warden. So the warden put Joseph in charge of all those held in the prison, and he was made responsible for all that was done there. The warden paid no attention to anything under Joseph's care, because the Lord was with Joseph and gave him success in whatever he did."

David was a promise driven person. After his anointing as king, he fought and killed the giant Goliath; he endured the jealousy of Saul, and resisted tempting opportunities to retaliate against who tried to kill him on more than one occasion; he lived as an outlaw in the very country over which he had been anointed king; he lived in a cave with people who were in debt, in distress and discontented. Yet because he handled his problems according to and consistent with God's promise, he eventually emerged as the king over all of Israel having achieved God's promise. 2nd Samuel 5:1-2, "All the tribes of Israel came to David at Hebron and said, we are your own flesh and blood. In the past while Saul was king over us, you were the one who led Israel on their military campaigns. And the Lord said to you, you will shepherd my people Israel and you will become their ruler."

David was the youngest (probably a teenager) of Jesse's eight sons, when God promised he would be king over all Israel. 1 Samuel 16:10-12, Jesse had seven of his sons pass before Samuel but Samuel said, "The Lord has not chosen these. Are these all the sons you have?" Jesse said, "There is still the youngest but he is tending sheep." Samuel said, "Send for him." When David showed up God said, "Rise and anoint him. He is the one." However, it wasn't until he had reached at least age thirty that the promise was achieved. 2 Samuel 5:3-5, "When all the elders of Israel came to King David at Hebron, the king made a compact with them before God and they anointed David king over Israel. David was thirty years old when he became king, and he reigned forty years. He reigned seven years over Judah and thirty-three years over all Israel."

There is always a price to pay for achieving your promise. But, your

promise is always worth much more than that price.

This is the step where expansion, promotion, enhancement and enlargement occur. This step is where the unexpected happens. It is where we are brought face to face with forces of resistance that are not within our control. Successful movement against resistance builds your strength, enhances your capacity, expands your authority, enlarges your territory and promotes your position. You know you're getting stronger, wiser, healthier and larger when you are not derailed or distracted from your promise by unexpected and unwanted adversity.

Expansion, enhancement and enlargement can occur only by successfully working against resistance. You are made stronger by each trial and trouble over which you triumph. Your authority is enhanced and expanded by each agony and anguish you overcome. Your territory is enlarged by successfully handling hardships at increasingly higher levels of difficulty.

No normal person looks for trouble, trial or hardship. But trial, trouble and hardship often find people driven by their promise. This is because promise driven people often find themselves struggling against the forces and powers that

251

prevent them from pushing toward their promise. Promise driven people are stronger, wiser, healthier and larger than purpose driven people because **promise reaches beyond purpose. The promise/dream/vision God gives to a person is always designed to help others as well. It's never just for that person. And because it has a wider and broader impact, it touches and challenges the status quo in some way.** The status quo never wants to let go. It always puts up resistance. And this resistance, when faced and overcome, expands, enhances and enlarges those who insist and persist in pursuing their promise.

You expand and enlarge your territory by taking on more challenging tasks. The human tendency seems to be to pursue the pathway of least resistance. People tend to favor the easy way, the quick way, the quick fix. We want many things, big things, expensive things. But, we want them right away. And not only do we want them right away, we want them at little to no cost financially, intellectually, physically and most importantly, spiritually. We want things but we don't want to have to go through anything to get them. We want success but we don't want to sacrifice. There seems to be a failure to appreciate that sacrifice always comes before success, even in the dictionary.

Don't seek the easy way. Develop the habit of taking the high road, the narrow road, the less traveled road. Take on the tough challenges. Seek out growth, development and strengthening experiences. That is, seek experiences in areas that you know little to nothing about, you've always had great difficulty with, or you've always been just plain afraid of.

Do a serious self-examination and identify those areas in your life where you know you have become comfortable and complacent. Examine whether or not and how these areas may be connected or related to your promise/dream/vision. If you have become comfortable and complacent in areas essential to the achievement of your promise, you will not achieve your promise. For example, if you are a gifted athlete or singer with the potential of being a national or world champion, but you have become comfortable or complacent about practice and training, you will never achieve your promise of being a national or world champion.

Promise is at the end of a path that includes the pain of serious and significant purging and pruning. In other words, **achieving promise means facing and dealing with the associated pain.** It is an oxymoron to think you can seek your promise and simultaneously seek to avoid pain. When you seek your promise, the pain along the path to promise is just something that must be faced and dealt with.

This step is why you must love and have passion for your promise. This step is where the pain comes. And, the pain comes because of what you must go through. It comes because you have to cut away from old friends who have become comfortable and complacent and have helped to make you comfortable and complacent. The pain comes because you have to cut back on things that are pleasurable and comforting in order to do the work of training and practice. Training and practice done at the appropriate level of intensity and frequency may be painful, but will grow you into your promise. Training and practice at the appropriate level of intensity and frequency will stretch you. And, in the stretching, you will experience pain.

No one likes pain. In fact, people go to great lengths to avoid pain. A low tolerance of pain is virtually a guarantee you will not achieve your promise. The irony of people having a low tolerance for the pain associated with reaching their promise is they virtually always experience pain on their chosen, lesser path. **Often the pain experienced on the path to promise turns out to be not as great as the pain eventually felt by those who decide not to pursue their promise.**

Since you will experience pain whether you pursue your promise or not, it makes total sense to me that the pain to experience should be that attached to your promise.

The purging and pruning processes involved in this refinement and enhancement step can be painful enough to make people change their minds about pursuing their promise. This is why God's blessing is required to achieve your promise. You must know and be convinced that God's blessing is on you. And of course, God's blessing is the guarantee that comes attached to His promise. God's blessing means God is with you. God being with you guarantees a victorious journey.

God's blessing comes with His Word, promise/dream/vision because God's blessing is needed to achieve the promise He gives. **Promise driven people operate at high levels of thought, behavior and results.** And it is at these levels that the greatest amount of resistance occurs. Thus, the need for God's blessing.

God's blessing is for where He wants to take you. It is for what He wants to do through you. It is future oriented. It is to enable or empower you to accomplish the word promise He has given you. God's blessing is God's hand or God's presence on and in your life.

Whatever God's hand touches always increases in productivity or fruitfulness. In other words, the blessing of God always leads to increased productivity

and fruitfulness. And, because of how difficult and challenging God's promises are, His blessing is needed to achieve the increased productivity and fruitfulness.

Several scriptures connect God's blessing to increased productivity and fruitfulness. Some of them include the following: "God blessed them and said, Be fruitful and increase in number and fill the water in the seas and let the birds increase on earth. (Genesis 1:22 NIV) God blessed them and said to them, Be fruitful and increase in number; fill the earth and subdue it. (Genesis 1:28 NIV) Then God blessed Noah and his sons, saying to them, Be fruitful and increase in number and fill the earth. (Genesis 9:1 NIV) God said to Abram, I will make you into a great nation and I will bless you; I will make your name great... I will bless those who bless you... and all peoples on earth will be blessed through you. (Genesis 12:2-3 NIV) God said of Sarah who was barren up to that point, I will bless her and will surely give you a son by her. I will bless her so that she will be the mother of nations; kings of peoples will come from her. (Genesis 17:16 NIV) God said of Ishmael, I will surely bless him; I will make him fruitful and will greatly increase his numbers." (Genesis 17:20 NIV)

In the 5th chapter of the book of Matthew, Jesus further outlines the connection between God's blessing and future increase. Jesus is saying in His collection of beatitudes that God blesses those who are poor in spirit with the increase of 'the kingdom of heaven.' He blesses those who are meek with the increase of 'inheriting the earth.' He blesses those who hunger and thirst after righteousness with the increase of 'being fulfilled.' He blesses those who endure persecution because of righteousness with the increase of 'the kingdom of heaven.'(Matthew 5:3,5,6,10 NIV)

When the angel Gabriel appeared to Mary he said, "Hail, thou who are highly favored, the Lord is with you; blessed are thou among women."(Luke 1:28 KJV) What Mary was being told was, God had for her an environment altering, paradigm shifting promise. And, His blessing – that is, God being with her – would be needed to achieve it.

Whom God touches is blessed. Whom God blesses is increased. Whom God increases is enlarged or enhanced.

Seven Days of Devotion to Expansion

Spiritual Principle to focus on is SELF-DISCIPLINE.

DAY 1: Reaching your promise requires struggling against the status quo.

Scripture: 1 Corinthians 15:58

Word for the Day: FIGHT

Other Scriptures: Galatians 6:9-10; 2 Timothy 4:7

Affirmations:
- "I am a fighter."
- "I am a finisher."
- "I will not give up."
- "I will keep pushing."

Suggested Activities:
- Identify an area of your life where you have accepted and become comfortable with the status quo (e.g. technological illiteracy, failing marriage relationship, excess weight, no exercise routine).
- Determine to, and declare you will turn it around.

- Work on it and change it over the next 49 days.
- Practice having conversations with God like you are conversing with a friend or neighbor.

Notes to myself:

<u>DAY 2</u>: Be prepared to handle any pain and suffering associated with your struggle/fight.

Scripture: 1 Corinthians 10:13

Word for the Day: ENDURE · PERSEVERE

Other Scriptures: 2 Peter 2:9; Romans 8:37
Psalm 30:5; 1 John 4:4
Philippians 4:13

Affirmations:
- "I am tough enough to take it."
- "I am tough enough."
- "I can handle this."
- "I can do all things through Christ who strengthens me."

Suggested Activities:
- First be clear that "toughness" is more spiritual and mental than physical.
- Meditate on and memorize the scriptures for this day.

Notes to myself:

<u>DAY 3</u>: Always be excellent. Always be and do things at your highest and best.

Scripture: 1 Corinthians 10:31

Word for the Day: EXCELLENCE

Other Scriptures: Colossians 3:17; 1 Peter 4:11

Affirmations:
- "I will glorify God with my behavior."
- "I will glorify God with my words."
- "I will be and do the best I can."

Suggested Activities:
- Prioritize things you don't like doing with #1 being the thing you least like to do. These things may be large or small, major or minor, simple or complicated. Your list may include for example: washing dishes, cleaning the garage, scrubbing floors, house cleaning, washing clothes, dealing with a certain difficult coworker or family member, cleaning your car inside and out.
- Pick something of high priority on the list.
- Practice doing the 'something' you selected at the level of your highest and best over the next 49 days.

- The greatest benefit will be derived from selecting something you least like.
- Repeat this process.

Notes to myself:

<u>DAY 4</u>: Promise driven people expect to expand.

Scripture: 1 John 5:4

Word for the Day: EXPECT VICTORY!

Other Scriptures: Philippians 4:13
Philippians 4:19; Hebrews 11:1

Affirmations:
- "I am an overcomer."
- "I expect to be victorious."

Suggested Activities:
- Remember, expectation impacts behavior in a way that is consistent with what is expected.
- Reflect on what behavior changes and how, when you are expecting:
  - a baby.
  - to be picked up.
  - to have to change your residence.
  - to change jobs.
  - company (family and friends visiting).
- Identify ongoing plans and/or projects that you expect to successfully complete.
- Examine whether or not your behavior is consistent with what is expected.

- If there is consistency, continue the behavior. If there is inconsistency, make the necessary change.

Notes to myself:

DAY 5: A path to promise transforms you.

Scripture: Romans 12:2

Word for the Day: TRANSFORMATION

Other Scriptures: Romans 12:1-2
Ephesians 4:20-24
2 Corinthians 5:17

Affirmations:
- "I am being transformed."
- "I am renewing my mind."
- "I am a new creation."

Suggested Activities:
- Practice seeing yourself in the context of God's promise for your life.
  - Visualize – in as much detail as possible – what will be happening when you reach your promise.
  - Do this at least three times a day over the next 49 days.
- Practice saying to yourself that:
  "I am who God says I am."
  "I am God's promise."
  "I can do what God says I can do."
  "I can achieve God's promise for my life."

- Do this simultaneously with the times you do your visualizations as listed above.

Notes to myself:

<u>DAY 6</u>: **Promise driven people are able to adapt.**

Scripture: Philippians 4:13

Word for the Day: FLEXIBILITY

Other Scriptures: John 1:1-4; Isaiah 55:9-11
Matthew 6:25-34
Philippians 4:11-13

Affirmations:
- "Expect the unexpected."
- "Blessed are the flexible for they shall never be bent out of shape."
- "The path to promise can be very unpredictable."
- "I will not let the unpredictable keep me from reaching what God has predicted/ promised for my life."
- "I may bend but I will not break."

Suggested Activity:
- Know that 'to adapt' is to be flexible. It is to adjust.
- Know that life adjusts/adapts. Anything that is rigid with no adjustment is dead.
- Reflect on and review the number of areas in your life that require frequent, unpredictable

adjustments to achieve success. For example:

relationships – marital and parental.
traffic.
weather.
loss.
gain.

Notes to myself:

DAY 7: Promise driven people behave and live like God is with them.

Scripture: Matthew 25:21

Word for the Day: BLESSED
ENLARGED TERRITORY

Other Scriptures: Hebrews 13:6
Philippians 4:12-13
Genesis 1:28, Judges 6:14-16
Luke 1:28, 1 Chronicles 4:9-10

Affirmations:
- "God is with me."
- "I am blessed."
- "I am blessed and highly favored."
- "God will never leave nor forsake me."

Suggested Activities:
- Practice behaving like you already have God's promise for your life.
- Over the next 49 days practice:
  being committed.
  being accountable.
  being prepared.
  being mature.
  being productive.
  behaving like you are ruler over many, or an 'enlarged territory'.

275

Notes to myself:

Step Seven: *Promise*

The vine bears much fruit and glorifies God.

Promise driven lives change the world.

Promise driven lives change the way things are done and the things that are done.

Promise driven lives produce paradigm shifts and create new paradigms.

Promise driven lives are productive in season and out of season, in good times and hard times. They do their best during the worst. They get the most from the least. While an outlaw, and living in a cave, David received and mentored hundreds of men in debt, distress and discontent, turning them into "mighty men" of God.

Promise driven lives are "faithful over a few things".

Promise driven people live at the highest levels. They live focused on positive outcomes and results. They live believing and

277

behaving like "they can". They live connected and yielded to a force much larger than themselves.

Promise driven people are engaged, energetic and enthusiastic.

Promise driven people are involved in making things happen. You will never find a promise driven person sitting on the sidelines of life.

Promise driven people don't wait for things to come to them. They go get them.

Promise driven lives are full, rich, involved and engaged. They are filled with experiences, rich with results, involved in making things happen and engaged with each moment in life.

Promise driven people make "higher level" decisions. They make decisions for the larger good of the larger number of people.

Promise driven people are problem solvers. They solve problems because they are always mindful of God's promise, which is the greater good for the greater number, no matter what the circumstances.

Promise driven people experience higher-level living. They experience more love, joy, peace, patience, and kindness and they have more righteousness, faith, humility and self-discipline. When you have higher level focus, (God's promise), higher level thinking and make higher level decisions (promise driven decisions), you are not bogged down, tripped up and stifled by the short-sightedness of self-centeredness.

Promise driven lives have large amounts of self-discipline. The discipline of self is the foundational key to achieving promise.

Promise driven lives experience more peace than others. This is not to say that promise driven people don't face conflict. They do. And, often they are faced with frequent, very large challenges. But, because of their focus on a higher agenda (God's promise) they are not as caught up in the frustration that results from the friction of haggling over small stuff.

Promise driven people experience more joy than others. This is because the concentration of promise driven people is at the heart of what brings people joy. Helping others, being kind to others, blessing others is always at the center of what promise driven people do. And these things bring joy.

Promise driven people are always cooperative and contributory, and not just when things go their way.

Promise driven people are always willing and ready to give to others what they can to help others reach for and achieve their dreams/visions/promise.

Seven Days of Devotion to Promise

Spiritual Principle to focus on is
HUMILITY · KINDNESS

DAY 1: I am committed to my promise.

Scripture: Mark 12:30

Word for the Day: COMMITMENT

Other Scriptures: John 3:16; 1 John 4:7-8

Affirmation:
- "I am committed to my promise."

Suggested Activity:
- Demonstrate love.

Notes to myself:

<u>DAY 2</u>: I am accountable to my promise.

Scripture: Hebrews 11:1

Word for the Day: ACCOUNTABILITY

Other Scriptures: Matthew 25:21

Affirmation:
- "I am accountable to my promise."

Suggested Activity:
- Demonstrate faith.

Notes to myself:

<u>DAY 3</u>: I will prepare for my promise.

Scripture: 1 Thessalonians 5:17

Word for the Day: PREPARATION

Other Scriptures: Galatians 6:7-9; Luke 14:25-30

Affirmation:
- "I will prepare for my promise."

Suggested Activity:
- Demonstrate patience.

Notes to myself:

<u>DAY 4</u>: I must be mature to reach and hold onto my promise.

Scripture: Matthew 5:48

Word for the Day: MATURITY

Other Scriptures: 1 Samuel 16:7

Affirmation:
- "I must be mature to reach and hold onto my promise."

Suggested Activity:
- Demonstrate righteousness and peace.

Notes to myself:

<u>DAY 5</u>: I am productive in my promise.

Scripture: Matthew 25:21

Word for the Day: PRODUCTIVE

Other Scriptures: Psalm 30:5

Affirmation:
- "I am productive in my promise."

Suggested Activity:
- Demonstrate joy.

Notes to myself:

<u>DAY 6</u>: God is with me on my journey to my promise. I am blessed.

Scripture: Hebrews 13:6

Words for the Day: ENLARGED TERRITORY

Other Scriptures: Genesis 1:28;
1 Chronicles 4:9-10

Affirmation:
- "God is with me on my journey to my promise. I am blessed."

Suggested Activity:
- Demonstrate self-discipline.

Notes to myself:

<u>DAY 7</u>: I will live my promise. I will live a promise driven life.

Scripture: John 1:14; 2 Corinthians 5:17

Word for the Day: PROMISE

Other Scriptures: John 1:1-14; Isaiah 55:9-11

Affirmations:
- "I will live my promise."
- "I will live a promise driven life."
- "I am a new creation."

Suggested Activity:
- Demonstrate humility and kindness.

Notes to myself:

VII. A BRIEF LOOK AT PROMISE DRIVEN ORGANIZATIONS

Promise driven organizations are higher agenda, high energy, environment altering organizations. They improve things. They make things better for others and themselves. They tackle big issues, big tasks and big challenges.

Promise driven organizations and institutions model and teach promise driven living. They help, assist and serve. They challenge, charge and change their atmosphere for the better all according to God's promise. By way of example, 'the church' is supposed to be God's organized earthly effort through which His people are facilitated in reaching His promise. The theory of the church is that it is God's word/promise in action here on earth.

In theory at least, any effort resulting in one life turning around and being supported in a godly direction, represents the purpose of the church. And each life, each soul, is important to the kingdom of God. However, the problem is the satisfaction resulting from the rejoicing over the one or few who have been converted. **The promise of God for His church is to reach everybody, everywhere. A promise driven church is**

never satisfied with "one or two being gathered in His name." A promise driven church is constantly going, constantly moving, constantly growing, constantly changing, constantly shifting, striving, working and reaching for God's promise to reach everybody, everywhere.

A promise driven church notices when things are stagnant and takes aggressive steps to make things happen. A promise driven church knows and understands the words of Jesus who said in Matthew 9:37, "The harvest is plentiful but the workers are few. Ask the Lord of the harvest, therefore to send out workers into His harvest field." In other words, Jesus was saying, there is always plenty to do to achieve the promise of God and, what was needed was, people driven by the promise of accomplishing the plenty.

A promise driven church is constantly and aggressively looking at how do we get to the next level? How do we get closer to our full potential? How do we get closer to God's promise?

A promise driven organization/church is blessed. This means God is with it. And, God has to be with it in order to facilitate the achievement of His promise. A promise driven church/organization is never static, stagnant, satisfied, comfortable, complacent, content, indifferent, uninvolved, uninterested or apathetic.

God blesses promise driven churches/ organizations. Churches/organizations that have and exhibit the courage, strength, boldness and daring to be driven by the promise/Word of God, are blessed by God. God's blessing is designed to facilitate the achievement of His promise.

In fact, I believe scripture not only suggests, but makes rather clear that God's blessing is for the stated purpose of empowering people to achieve His promise that is yet to occur. In other words, **God blesses for where He's taking people. God blesses for a journey. God blesses for where you are going. God's blessing is for your future that is stated in your present. God's blessing is God's favor necessary for you to achieve the future (promise) God has given you.**

God's blessing is necessary to achieve God's promise. This is because God's promise is so much bigger, better and beyond where you are. So, God must be with you to achieve His promise. God's blessing is God's way of saying, "I will be with you." It also says, "You're going to need Me to be with you." And finally, God's blessing says, "I am with you not only to help you but to guarantee that you succeed."

Genesis 1:28 says God blessed them (man and woman) and said to them, "Be fruitful and increase in number. Fill the earth and subdue it. Rule over the fish of the sea, birds of the air and every living creature that moves on the ground."(NIV) God blessed humankind because His blessing was necessary to achieve His promise. God blessed humans because He needed for them to know that He would be with them to help and guarantee that they would indeed "exercise dominion, be fruitful, increase, replenish and managed the earth."

Genesis 12:2-3 describes how Abram is blessed by God for the journey God is asking him to take. God's promise to Abram is, "I will make you into a great nation. I will bless you. I will make your name great. You will be a blessing. I will bless those who bless you." Abram's principle or "if" is, "Leave your country, your people, and your father's house and go to the land I will show you."(Genesis 12:1 NIV) Abram's promise/vision/dream was much more than just a change of residence. He was being asked to reinvent himself. He was being asked to have his life transformed into something totally different and new. He was being asked to make not just geographical changes, but also changes that were spiritual, educational, economical, philosophical, social, political, cultural, intellectual and emotional.

To achieve God's promise, your total being is impacted. You can't reach the promise of God with a finger, a hand, an arm or a leg. The promise of God is for your whole self, impacts your whole self

and can only be reached by your whole self. And, as such, the promise of God requires the blessing of God to be achieved. God was saying to Abram, 'I will bless you' because My blessing is needed, will help you, and guarantees you will achieve My promise. With God, His blessing is His promise. His promise is a blessing.

Another example of the future orientation of God's blessing is what the angel says to Mary in Luke 1:28(KJV) "...Hail thou that are highly favored, the Lord is with you: blessed art thou among women." **The favor and blessing of God on and in your life is to ensure your achievement of God's promise for your life.** And God's promise – as it was for Mary – is so much bigger, better and beyond where you are that God's blessing presence is necessary for its accomplishment. These examples of how God responds to individuals who live promise driven lives reflect how God responds to organizations/churches that are driven by His promise.

Acts 4:33 explains the favor, grace and blessing of God that resulted for the newly established church/organization that had the strength, courage, daring and boldness to live the promise driven lives that made them the greatest possible witness/ evidence for God. Further explanation of what results when the organized body of God's people decide to live their lives according to His Word/

promise is found in the first thirteen verses of the 28th chapter of the book of Deuteronomy: "If you fully obey the LORD your God and carefully follow all his commands I give you today, the LORD your God will set you high above all the nations on earth. All these blessings will come upon you and accompany you if you obey the LORD your God: You will be blessed in the city and blessed in the country. The fruit of your womb will be blessed, and the crops of your land and the young of your livestock—the calves of your herds and the lambs of your flocks. Your basket and your kneading trough will be blessed. You will be blessed when you come in and blessed when you go out. The LORD will grant that the enemies who rise up against you will be defeated before you. They will come at you from one direction but flee from you in seven. The LORD will send a blessing on your barns and on everything you put your hand to. The LORD your God will bless you in the land he is giving you. The LORD will establish you as his holy people, as he promised you on oath, if you keep the commands of the LORD your God and walk in his ways. Then all the peoples on earth will see that you are called by the name of the LORD, and they will fear you. The LORD will grant you abundant prosperity—in the fruit of your womb, the young of your livestock and the crops of your ground—in the land he swore to your forefathers to give you. The LORD will open the heavens, the storehouse of his bounty, to send rain on your land in season and to bless all the work of your hands. You will lend to many nations but will borrow from none. The LORD will make you the head, not the tail. If you pay attention to the commands of the LORD your God that I give you this day and carefully follow them, you will always be at the top, never at the bottom."(NIV)

The blessings listed in Deuteronomy 28 are God's promises for those who practice the principles attached to them. The promises of God always come with God's blessing. This is because – as already stated – God's promise can only be achieved with God's blessing.

Promise driven organizations are integrous. They live the message they bring. They don't say one thing and do another. They do as Jesus did. They spread the Gospel by precept and example, by teaching and demonstrating, by lecture and laboratory, by explaining and experimenting, by their talk and their walk, with their lips and their life. In other words, promise driven organizations are live demonstration models of God's Word/promise in action.

They are involved in and positively impact what's happening around them. They operate from the perspective of, 'our presence will make a positive difference.' **Promise driven**

organizations/churches are heard from on the issues of the day. They have a voice. Their voice is one of victory for righteousness, love, kindness, humility, peace, joy, faith, patience and self-discipline. Their voice is sought after by policy-makers and their voice seeks after problem makers. People know they are present and accounted for. No one has to wonder where they are, what they are doing or what they stand for. When they speak, people listen because what they say, they do and, what they do is always beneficial to the people being served.

Promise driven organizations/churches can be run only by promise driven people. And promise driven people are people with a specific vision/dream. They are committed to this vision and are willing to be held accountable for it. They are prepared for this vision and they are continuously growing, developing, moving on and maturing in it. They are productive in their vision as they are always outcome and results oriented. And, they know, understand, even appreciate that the problems, pain, adversity, hardship, trial and trouble that are often prelude to promise, all serve to expand and enlarge us to handle the promise.

CONCLUSION

Each of us is born with promise. In fact, every birth is the manifestation of promise. Promise is the word, idea, concept or thought that must be materialized into existence, substance and reality. We are all born with promise. And then, from birth we must contend with the forces of death, which are constantly coming against life and its full manifestation. This is why God's help is required to achieve your promise. And God's help begins with the knowledge that God is the giver of His promise.

God's promise, as great and challenging as it always is, comes with a guarantee. God guarantees the achievement of the promise He gives. This point then, raises questions. If God gives us our promise/dream/vision with a guarantee, why do so few achieve it? If God is almighty and His Word/promise "never returns to Him void" why don't more people achieve their promise/dream/vision? Why do so many people go to their grave with their music/song/promise/dream/vision still in them? The answer is simple. The problem is not with God or His Word. The problem is with people who decide not to believe God or His Word/promise/dream/vision.

Those who decide to believe in God and His Word are the ranks from which promise driven people come. There are many in scripture who achieve their purpose of believing in and worshipping God. But, the flow and direction of scripture revolves around those who are driven by God's promise.

Promise driven people determine the many directions of the many stories in, and the direction of the main story of the Bible. We know the names of the promise driven people. We study the stories of the promise driven people. We learn the lessons from the lives of the promise driven people. But, too many of us stop short of seeing ourselves as today's promise driven people. God's Word is and has been applicable to all people, in all places, of all time periods. The point of scripture is that we are today's Noah, Abraham, Joseph, Moses, Joshua, Caleb, David, Solomon, Samuel, Elijah, Elisha, Daniel, Peter, James, John, Paul, Sarah, Naomi, Ruth, Rahab, Deborah, Hanah, Elizabeth, Mary, Abigail, Ester, Vashti, Dorcas, Anna, Priscilla, Martha, Mary, Lazarus and Jesus.

None of these, except Jesus, were perfect but all of them were impacted and driven by God's Word/promise. We know their names. We've studied their stories. Their lives, as they were driven by God's Word/promise (Jesus), shaped the course of the Bible.

We are here today to shape the course of the world in which we live. We have been given that promise. The promise

comes with a guarantee. The decision to live a promise driven life is ours.

Scripture makes it clear that we are born with promise. Jeremiah 1:5 says, "Before I formed you in the womb I knew you, before you were born I set you apart; I appointed you as a prophet to the nations."(NIV) Isaiah 49:1 says, "Listen to me, you islands; hear this you distant nations: Before I was born the Lord called me; from my birth He has mentioned my name."(NIV) Isaiah 44:24 says, "This is what the Lord says – your redeemer who formed you in the womb."(NIV) Isaiah 44:2, "This is what the Lord says – he who made you, who formed you in the womb, and who will help you."(NIV) Galations 1:15 says, "But when God who set me apart from birth and called me by His grace, was pleased to reveal His son in me so that I might preach Him among the Gentiles..."(NIV) Luke 1:30-33 says, "The angel said to Mary, don't be afraid, you have found favor with God. You will be with child and give birth to a son, and you are to give him the name Jesus. He will be great and will be called the Son of the Most High. The Lord God will give him the throne of his father David, and he will reign over the house of Jacob forever; his kingdom will never end."(NIV)

We are born with promise. The promise is from God. The promise comes with a guarantee from God. The decision to live a promise driven life is ours. Many

before us, including and especially Jesus the Christ, made their decision. We owe a debt to promise driven people who came before us and those who will come after us. That debt can be paid by our decision to become promise driven people.